D0410286

WITHDRAWN

Tropical
aquarium

Tropical
aquarium

Sean Evans

EDINBURGH
CITY
LIBRARIES

THE CITY OF EDINBURGH COUNCIL

C0024325465

Bertrams	25.08.06
SF 457	£17.99
NT	AH1

- 7 AUG 2006

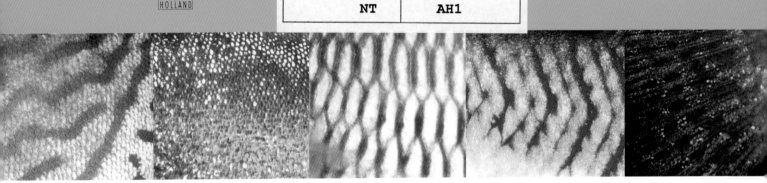

First published in 2006 by

New Holland Publishers

London • Cape Town • Sydney • Auckland

www.newhollandpublishers.com

86 Edgware Rd
London W2 2EA
United Kingdom

80 McKenzie Street
Cape Town 8001
South Africa

14 Aquatic Drive
Frenchs Forest,
NSW 2086
Australia

218 Lake Road
Northcote,
Auckland
New Zealand

Copyright © 2006 New Holland Publishers (UK) Ltd

Copyright © 2006 in text: Sean Evans

Copyright © 2006 in illustrations: Bronwyn Lusted

Copyright © 2006 in photography: refer to p160

All rights reserved. No part of this publication may be
reproduced, stored in a retrieval system or transmitted, in
any form or by any means, electronic, mechanical, photo-
copying, recording or otherwise, without the prior written
permission of the publishers and copyright holders.

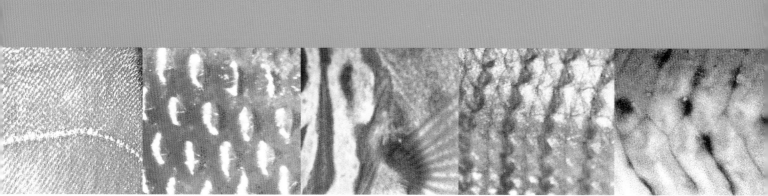

Publishing managers: Claudia Dos Santos, Simon Pooley

Commissioning editor: Alfred LeMaitre

Editor: Katja Splettstoesser

Designer: Elmari Kuyler

Illustrator: Bronwyn Lusted

Picture researcher: Tamlyn Beaumont-Thomas

Proofreader/Indexer: Sylvia Grobbelaar

Production: Myrna Collins

ISBN: 1 84537 161 5 (HB)

         1 84537 162 3 (PB)

Reproduction by Resolution Colours (Pty) Ltd, Cape Town,
South Africa

Printed and bound in Singapore by Tien Wah Press (Pte) Ltd

10 9 8 7 6 5 4 3 2 1

Contents

PART I SETTING UP AND MAINTAINING
AN AQUARIUM

PART II   TROPICAL FISH SPECIES GUIDE

Introduction

Keeping fish is an incredibly popular pastime around the world. Exactly what makes it so popular is difficult to define, and no doubt the motivations vary from one person to the next.

Many people are fascinated by the wonders of nature in general. Perhaps fish hold an extra level of wonder for them because the underwater world is separate and different to our own, and we can only enter it by using specialized equipment.

Some people are motivated by the relaxing influence of a fish tank. There is no shortage of evidence that watching fish swim serenely about their underwater world lowers stress levels – little wonder that aquaria have become increasingly popular in places such as doctors' and dentists' waiting rooms.

Perhaps another factor in the wide appeal of keeping fish lies in the fact that people can enjoy fish at so many different levels: many fishkeepers may be content with a single tank that forms a nice focal point in their living room. They tend to limit their involvement in the hobby to an occasional visit to the local aquatic shop while others may find themselves absorbed into the world of fishkeeping on a much deeper level than they ever expected, which often leads to additional tanks appearing around the home! To them, fishkeeping is both an art and a science. Creating an attractive aquarium

can bring out an artistic flair, but for those who enjoy learning more about their hobby, there is more information to be found relating to the many fish species available than anyone could hope to absorb in a lifetime.

Keeping fish leads many people to new areas of knowledge; those who have never shown any particular interest in plants or gardening might find themselves creating stunning underwater planted aquascapes. Others may find themselves wanting to know more about the areas their fish come from – faraway lakes and rivers – so that they might more accurately recreate these environments in the aquarium. This interest might even culminate in a trip to such places, or even trying their hand at snorkelling or scuba diving.

Whatever your level of involvement in keeping aquarium fish, I hope that you get some measure of the enjoyment from it that I have experienced over the years.

Above: A tropical aquarium can be simply an attractive focal point in the home, or a stunningly beautiful slice of nature.

Setting Up & Maint

aining an Aquarium

Water Chemistry and Quality

The water in aquaria is complex due to substances dissolved or suspended in it and the way these can alter over time. The terms 'water chemistry' and 'water quality' are used interchangeably in fishkeeping. Water chemistry covers the physical and chemical properties of water, while water quality refers to the properties of water concerned directly with the health of fish.

The concept of water quality is sometimes misunderstood in that a novice fishkeeper might be heard to say: "My water quality is fine, it's crystal clear." Unfortunately, the clarity of water has little to do with its quality when it comes to maintaining healthy fish. Sparkling clear water can contain a deadly level of invisible dissolved waste products, whereas murky water (as found in many natural environments) may be perfectly safe from a biological point of view. The only way to confirm the quality of the water is to use appropriate test kits.

Temperature

Temperature is the most apparent water parameter, and also the easiest to measure and control. The optimum temperature value for tropical fish species lies somewhere between 20-30°C (68-86°F), therefore, a good middle value that suits the majority of tropical fish in a mixed aquarium is 25°C (77°F). The temperature of the water also affects other parameters such as the level of dissolved oxygen, and the rate at which fish produce and break down waste.

Left: Always use a thermometer to monitor the temperature of the aquarium — never rely solely on the setting on the heating device.

pH

In its simplest definition, pH is a measure of how acid or alkaline the water is. A more scientific definition of pH is that it refers to a measure of the concentration of hydrogen ions (H+) hence the uppercase 'H' in pH.

The pH scale runs from 0 to 14. A pH 7 is referred to as neutral (neither acidic nor alkaline). A pH below 7 is acidic, while a pH reading above 7 is alkaline. The majority of freshwater fish do not tolerate extremely acidic or alkaline water, so the desired pH range should be as close to neutral as possible.

The pH is affected constantly by processes within the aquarium such as aeration, the breakdown of wastes and plant metabolism. For this reason, it is important to check pH on a regular basis. The pH of your tank water is determined largely by your source water. For most fishkeepers, this means tap water. You may find that the pH at which your aquarium settles may not suit the pH requirements of your fish. In some cases, this may affect the type of fish you can keep.

Before attempting to change the pH of aquarium water, ask yourself if it is really necessary to do so. The pH range quoted for a given species is often based on its native waters. Although you might desire to mimic these conditions, the fish may be quite capable of thriving at a slightly different pH. It is also worth considering that many fish acquired as pets have been aquarium bred for generations and may have become accustomed to water conditions quite different to their natural habitat (this does not mean though that they have 'adapted' in the long-term biological sense).

Providing a stable pH is more important than attaining an exact pH value, as long as you avoid extremes. In most cases, your local aquarium store will be using water from the same supply as your own, which makes it easier for new fish to acclimatize to the water chemistry in your tank. If you do decide to alter your aquarium pH, do so carefully and slowly. Commercial pH-adjusting products can have disastrous consequences if used incorrectly.

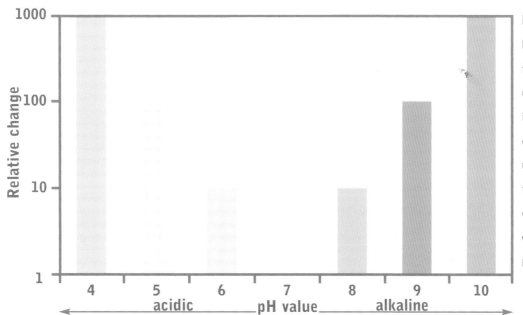

The logarithmic nature of the pH scale

Left: The pH scale is logarithmic, which means that a change of 1 pH unit is a 10-fold change in the hydrogen ion concentration that determines pH. This means that relatively small changes can have major effects — always adjust pH gradually.

13

Hardness

Water hardness relates to the amount of dissolved minerals in the water, and is usually referred to in units of degrees or parts-per-million (mg/litre). Most people are familiar with the concept of 'hard' water – meaning that it is difficult to produce lather with soap, as opposed to 'soft' water, where it is much easier. This is not due to *all* of the minerals in the water, but only certain ones which impart the property known as hardness. These are commonly split into two different measurements: General Hardness (GH), which measures mainly calcium and magnesium ions, and Carbonate Hardness (KH), which measures carbonate and bicarbonate ions.

An aquarium GH test kit measures calcium and magnesium ions (other minor ions can be involved, but they are not significant in fresh water). Other dissolved minerals such as sodium and potassium are not measured by a GH kit. Hence sodium choride does *not* harden water, as sometimes stated. Although the GH parameter does not measure all of the ions in the water, it is usually a good indication of the total mineral levels.

The level of minerals in the water can be important to fish for a number of reasons, not least of all because fish have to retain a certain balance between the minerals in their bodies and those in the water around them. Hardness can be important in specific scenarios such as when breeding fish. It should never be altered suddenly, and fish should not be transferred between tanks with extreme differences in hardness. However, as long as the hardness is stable, then a reasonable range is well tolerated by most fish. Carbonate hardness, usually abbreviated to KH, is essentially equivalent to 'alkalinity', a term more widely used in marine fishkeeping. Although the two terms are not exactly equivalent, they both refer to the ability of water to resist pH changes, that is, its 'buffering' capacity (or 'acid-neutralizing capacity').

What this means to the fishkeeper is that the higher the KH, the more stable the pH will be, and the more difficult it will be to change. A lower KH means the pH is potentially less stable. KH values of less than 3 degrees (or approx 50ppm) will mean that the pH could potentially 'crash' to a much lower value. However, regular water changes and avoiding overstocking or overfeeding can help prevent this. Aquarium water tends to acidify naturally over time, due to the breakdown of wastes. This can result in a reduction in the related KH and pH values. If the KH is close to zero, the pH can drop very suddenly.

If your source water has a low KH and you wish to make it more stable (or increase it for fish from hard, alkaline waters), this can be done by adding materials that release hardening salts (such as calcium carbonate) into the water. These could be limestone-based rocks such as tufa rock, coral sand or gravel mixed with the aquarium substrate,

Left: Internal filter box filters can be useful for adding specialized media such as peat for lowering pH and hardness.

Water hardness: terms and conversions

mg/l CaCO3 (PPM)	Degrees of Hardness	Described as:
0-50	0-3	soft
50-100	3-6	fairly soft
100-200	6-12	slightly hard
200-300	12-18	moderately hard
300-540	18-30	hard
540 +	30+	very hard

or calcium-based substrates added to a compartment in the filter. Increasing KH will also increase pH in most cases.

If you wish to reduce GH and KH, then peat or water-softening resins can be added to the filter. However, the best method is to dilute the harder water with almost pure water such as reverse osmosis (RO) or de-ionized (DI) water. This works on a simple dilution factor, i.e if you use dilute water with hardness of 10 degress 50:50 with pure water, the resulting hardness will be 5 degrees.

In the past some sources have tended to treat KH as if it were a component of GH. This is misleading and incorrect, as it is possible for the KH reading to exceed GH (as it does naturally in Lakes Malawi and Tanganyika). Part of this confusion stems from older aquarium literature referring to hardness as measuring all ions present in the water. However, this definition bears no relation to what hobbyists measure with a GH kit, and is best forgotten. Measurements such as total dissolved solids (TDS) and salinity can be made, but these are not normally of concern to most freshwater fishkeepers.

Left: A GH kit for testing water hardness.
Right: pH kit and pH adjustment solutions.

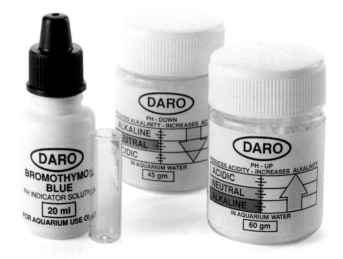

The Nitrogen Cycle – Ammonia, Nitrite and Nitrate

It is certainly no exaggeration to say that the nitrogen cycle is the single most important factor relating to fish health in aquaria. Imbalanced nitrogen levels are almost certainly responsible, directly or indirectly, for more stress and loss of fish than any other factor.

Fish waste, uneaten food and decaying plant matter all lead to the generation of ammonia in the aquarium. Fish also expel a large amount of waste ammonia through their gills in much the same way that we (and fish) breathe out carbon dioxide. Ammonia is very toxic to fish and can damage gills permanently. Even very low levels of ammonia, barely detectable with test kits, can cause stress and long-term damage if fish are exposed to them for prolonged periods. The actual amount of toxic ammonia present in an aquarium is dependant on water pH, and to a lesser extent, temperature. This is because, at acid pH-values, ammonia is in the form of less-toxic ammonium (NH_4). This, in turn, changes to the more toxic ammonia (NH_3) as the water becomes increasingly alkaline, thus a given level of ammonia/ammonium is more harmful in alkaline water. Luckily, there are naturally-occurring bacteria that convert NH_3 into a slightly less toxic compound, known as nitrite. This, too, is very harmful to fish if it builds up, but a second set of bacteria converts nitrite to nitrate, which is less toxic.

In a newly setup aquarium, there are not enough of these useful bacteria to cope with the waste levels and toxic ammonia can rise to dangerous levels. Eventually, the number of bacteria increases to cope with the ammonia, the ammonia level falls, and nitrite begins to build up. As the second type of bacteria increases, the nitrite is converted to the much less toxic nitrate.

This can take four to six weeks, although the precise time is affected by a number of factors. Once this has occurred, the aquarium is often referred to as cycled, or sometimes as mature – though the time taken for an aquarium to become more fully mature and stable is typically longer, about six months. It is therefore important to take steps to minimize the stress to fish and to prevent their loss during the initial cycling time of a new aquarium. These include:

- Adding only a few hardy fish at first, and monitoring ammonia and nitrite levels to ensure they are zero before adding any more fish.

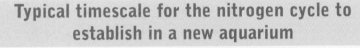

Typical timescale for the nitrogen cycle to establish in a new aquarium

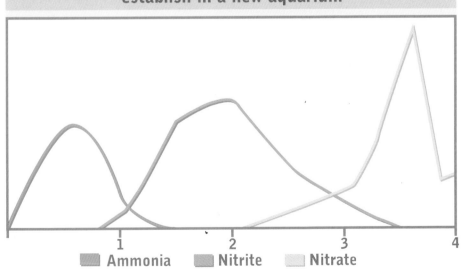

Ammonia   Nitrite   Nitrate

Left: It takes time for the nitrogen cycle to begin to function in a newly setup aquarium, typically around four weeks or more. Sufficient bacteria must build up to convert ammonia to nitrite, and then nitrite to nitrate.

- Feeding lightly, to minimize waste.
- If possible, obtaining some filter material, gravel/sand, plants or other décor from a mature aquarium that has been running for at least a few months. This will help to introduce necessary bacteria and speed up the cycling process. A fishkeeping friend or local store might be able to help with this.
- Cycling the tank before adding the fish. This requires an alternative source of ammonia to feed bacteria and start the maturing process. You could add small amounts of fish food daily, which is left to break down, or a pure ammonia source (plain household ammonia with no additives). If you use this latter method, you must monitor ammonia and nitrite levels carefully throughout. (Note that this method can take a long time unless you seed the tank with material from a mature aquarium.)
- Planting heavily about a week before adding any fish, and then stocking slowly. Plants not only introduce some important bacteria by means of their leaves and roots, they also take up ammonia and other wastes. (It is possible to avoid a noticeable cycle in a well planted tank that is stocked slowly.)

Once the initial maturing period is complete, ammonia and nitrite levels should remain at zero essentially – you should not be able to detect them with a standard aquarium test kit. There are certain factors, however, that can cause spikes of ammonia and/or nitrite even in mature tanks. These include:

- Filter failure caused by a fault, a lack of maintenance or a power cut.
- Overenthusiastic cleaning of 'biological' filter media, particularly in chlorinated tap or hot water.

Above: Overfeeding fish is a common cause of water quality problems, and could result in ammonia/nitrite spikes and elevated nitrate levels.

- The addition of too many fish at the same time.
- Overfeeding the fish.
- The use of medication either in excess or in combination with other medication.

In a mature and stable aquarium, ammonia and nitrite will be efficiently converted to nitrate. Although nitrate is less toxic, it can still become harmful if concentrations become very high. There is still much to learn about nitrate toxicity, and it is clear that different species have different levels of sensitivity.

Exposing fish to high nitrate levels over the long-term lowers their resistance to disease and affects their growth rate and ability to breed. More immediate problems may occur when transferring fish from a relatively low nitrate level (at the local fish store, for example) to a high nitrate level. This may lead to loss of new fish within a few days, even though they may appear fine. (The fish already in the tank have had time to gradually become accustomed to the increasing nitrate levels, whereas the newly introduced fish have not.) You should therefore aim to keep the level of nitrate in your tanks as low as possible, using regular partial water changes.

Chlorine and Chloramine

It is the responsibility of local water authorities to make sure your water supply is fit for human consumption, rather than ideal for use with aquarium fish. For this reason, they add chlorine to tap water to disinfect it. While the chlorine makes the tap water safe for us to drink, it makes it less suitable for use in the aquarium because chlorine is harmful to fish and other aquatic life. Low levels of this additive can cause stress and gill damage – high levels can be fatal. You must therefore treat any tap water, or other chlorinated source of water to be used for aquaria, prior to using it.

You can remove chlorine fairly easily by a number of different methods. One method is to simply aerate the water for about 24 hours prior to use. Another commonly used method is to add a commercial dechlorinator or water conditioner. They have traditionally been based on sodium thiosulphate, which neutralizes the chlorine. Some water conditioners contain extra ingredients that either bind with toxic heavy metals or add a protective slime layer to the fish. Filtration through activated carbon also removes chlorine. If you use this method, carry it out in a separate container with fresh carbon for at least 24 hours, before adding the water to the tank.

Some water authorities use chloramine, a compound of chlorine and ammonia, because it is a more stable disinfectant than chlorine alone. Traditional dechlorinators based on sodium thiosulphate neutralize the chlorine, but this releases ammonia. This could be dangerous or stressful for the fish, as it takes time for the biofiltration to convert the ammonia. If you know that your local water authority uses chloramine (or you are unsure of whether they do or not), select a new water conditioner product that neutralizes chlorine, and also converts ammonia into a non-toxic form.

Dissolved Gases

Only a certain amount of oxygen can dissolve from air into water, and this is dependant on temperature. In freshwater at 25°C (77°F), the maximum amount of oxygen that dissolves is about 8.1 milligrams per litre. Keep the oxygen level in the aquarium close to this saturation value. (In practice, fishkeepers rarely check oxygen levels, although test kits are available.) This can be achieved through:

- Good circulation and aeration by means of aquarium filters, circulation pumps and any additional aeration devices, which you should check regularly. This will ensure that sufficient oxygen enters the water surface from the air.

- Using a wide and shallow tank with a greater surface area. (The surface area of the aquarium is an important factor in determining the rate at which oxygen can enter the aquarium.) Such a tank will safely support more fish than a tall and narrow tank of the same volume.

- Using a spray bar or airstone or directing the filter outputs along the surface in order to agitate it effectively. This also increases the surface area of the water, which ensures high oxygen levels.

Note that overstocking and/or overfeeding can lead to declining oxygen levels. Oxygen levels below the saturation value can cause fish long-term low-level stress, which is likely to make them more susceptible to disease. If the oxygen levels are significantly less than the saturation value, fish may be seen to gasp near the surface. If oxygen levels fall as low as 2mg/l, fish may die.

Another consideration is that the conversion (oxidation) of ammonia to nitrite and then nitrate is dependant on oxygen. Low oxygen levels will reduce the efficiency of the biofilter, potentially leading to further water quality problems. In planted aquaria, plants use a small amount of oxygen for respiration at night, but during the daytime, this depletion is outweighed by the oxygen produced by photosynthesis. Because photosynthesis stops at night, oxygen levels tend to drop overnight in planted aquaria (the same phenomenon often occurs in non-planted aquaria, due to the presence of algae). For this reason, the effects of low oxygen levels are more likely to occur early in the morning.

The respiration of fish (and plants) on a continual basis produces carbon dioxide. If carbon dioxide levels become excessive, the fish will exhibit symptoms similar to oxygen shortage. Circulation and aeration in the aquarium helps to dispel some of the carbon dioxide from the water. As plants require carbon dioxide for photosynthesis, it is undesirable to expel the carbon dioxide too vigorously with additional airstones or excessive surface agitation in planted tanks. Indeed, carbon dioxide is often added to planted tanks to boost plant growth. However, the addition of carbon dioxide is normally stopped at night, when the plants are no longer using it for photosynthesis, to avoid an excessive build-up.

Below: Fish gasping at the surface could indicate a severe oxygen shortage, or a build-up of carbon dioxide. Aerate the water vigorously to correct these problems.

The Tank

The main factors affecting your choice of tank are likely to include the space you have available to position the tank, and your budget. However, it is also wise to do some advance planning on what sort of fish you would like to keep. It's not uncommon for new fishkeepers to select a small tank (often marketed as 'ideal for the beginner'), only to find themselves limited in their choice of fish and wishing they had opted for a larger tank.

Aim for the largest tank that your space and budget allows. Apart from a wider potential choice of fish, larger tanks have another disctinct advantage: stability. A larger volume of water is more stable in terms of parameters such as temperature. As conditions change more gradually in a larger volume of water, things are much less likely to go wrong suddenly.

A tank in the region of 90cm (36") long, 30cm (12") wide and 45cm (18") high is a good size for a first tank aimed at keeping the commonly available smaller tropical fish. The cost of a slightly larger tank does not increase that much, from say a 60cm (24") to a 90cm (36") tank. The equipment needed is essentially the same, and the increase in price for a slightly larger heater or light unit, for example, is often minimal.

One of the main decisions in choosing your tank will be whether to go for a systemized tank that comes complete with a hood, lighting and filter system – or a plain tank, to which you can add the required equipment of your choice.

Both of these have their plus and minus points. If you are a newcomer to fishkeeping, you may find it easier to opt for a systemized tank, which includes the necessary equipment in one package, rather than selecting it separately. Either way, a bit of background reading and the help of a good retailer should be able to help you in your selection. A good retailer will take the time to explain the plus points of a particular brand of tank or piece of equipment, rather than being in a hurry to make the sale.

A potential downside to a commercial systemized aquarium is lack of flexibility. It may not be easy to add extra equipment, or tailor it to your needs. In particular, the filtration system may be inadequate, or the lighting may be unsuitable for growing plants.

While there are many excellent designs of commercial systemized aquaria available, more experienced fishkeepers may wish to select the tank and the equipment to go with it individually. This allows the selection to be tailored towards a specific use. For example, heavy-duty filtration for cichlid tanks, or enhanced lighting for heavily planted aquaria.

A number of manufacturers produce a range of standard tanks. Larger retail outlets may also manufacture their own standard and custom sizes. The advantage of a custom-built tank is the flexibility to choose the exact size (and possibly shape) of the tank.

The thickness of glass is a very important factor in tank design. It is wise to use 6mm glass as a minimum thickness for tank construction, though small commercial tanks are sometimes manufactured from 4mm glass. In general, tanks more than 45cm (18") high will need to be constructed of at least 8mm, or preferably 10mm glass. Tank depths greater than 60cm (24") usually require 12mm glass. Above 75-100cm (30-39"), the thicker glass required is both extremely heavy and very expensive, and usually requires a custom build-on-site project.

A number of commercial tanks are manufactured in acrylic, especially those with fancy shapes. Acrylic is relatively light and strong, but does scratch more easily. It is also significantly more expensive than glass for larger aquaria.

Position

Although natural sunlight can have a pleasant visual effect in an aquarium, it is not wise to position the tank near a window where it will receive direct sunlight. The rich spectrum of sunlight encourages excessive algal growth. Excessive heat may also be a problem for the same reason, so do not place the tank near a heater. Also, avoid locations subject to cold draughts, any noise, vibration or excessive people traffic.

You also need to position your tank on a purpose-built stand or cabinet; use one that has been specifically designed to hold an aquarium or other sturdy item of furniture. Water is very heavy — 1kg per litre or approximately 10lb per imperial gallon. This means that a tank of 120 x 45 x 60cm (48 x 18 x 24in) would weigh in the region of 300kg (660lb), which is more than a quarter of a metric tonne! For very large tanks, you may need to have a structural engineer check your floor.

Right: Always check that the tank is level before committing to the setup process. If the tank is not supported evenly on a firm surface, it could lead to stress on the joints, which could cause the tank to leak.

Heating & Lighting

Heating

To keep tropical fish healthy you need to maintain your aquarium within a constant temperature range. The temperature requirements of individual species vary, and you should check these for any fish you intend to keep. For most tropical species, the optimum lies between 22-28°C (72-82°F), with 25°C (77°F) being a common compromise.

The heater-wattage requirement for a particular aquarium depends on a number of factors, including the ambient temperature of the room and the specific size of your aquarium. Allow at least 1watt per litre or 4.5 watts per imperial gallon, rounding up to the nearest available heater size. A tank of 180l (40 imperial gallons) for example, requires 180 watts, so you would use the next standard heater size of 200W.

The most common heating devices available on the market for aquariums include:

- Combined heater-stats that are by far the most common way of heating an aquarium because they incorporate both the heating element and the thermostat control into a rod-shaped device. These are widely available in standard wattages from 25W to 300W or more, usually in gradients of 25 or 50W.

Heater-stats are usually completely submersible, but check the manufacturer's instructions first.

- A thermofilter is an alternative to using a separate in-tank heater, which combines filtration and heating in one unit. Some internal filters incorporate a heater into their designs, which minimizes the equipment visible in the tank and keeps everything neat. Some external-canister filters also have a heating element incorporated into their designs.

- Another suggestion is an in-line heater fitted into the return pipe of a standard external filter.

To provide constant heat when using in-tank heaters, ensure that there is sufficient water flowing around the heater and that it is not in direct contact with the substrate, décor or aquarium glass.

Above: The lighting above a tank allows us to appreciate the fish's colours at their best. In a planted tank, it provides the light needed for photosynthesis.

Opposite: Combined heater-stats are the most common way to heat an aquarium and are usually fully submersible.

For large aquaria, use two or more small heaters to achieve the required total wattage. Place these at opposite ends of the tank to provide constant heat. Using two or more heaters also provides backup; should a heater fail in the 'off' position, the other heater will prevent the temperature dropping quickly, allowing you time to notice the problem.

Always use a separate thermometer to verify whether the setting on the heater is producing the desired aquarium temperature. Check the thermometer regularly, such as at feeding times each day. Modern heating devices are generally reliable, but it is advisable to seek a well-known and trusted brand, and it is worth paying a little extra for this.

If you need to remove the heater from an aquarium or lower the water level during maintenance, make sure the heater is switched off at least 10 minutes in advance. Allow the heater to cool before removing it from the water, otherwise it could crack.

Lighting

The lighting in an aquarium serves a number of functions. Firstly, it allows us to view and appreciate the fish more fully than would be possible indoors in natural daylight. More importantly, it provides a natural day-and-night cycle for the fish. Lighting becomes more critical if living plants are incorporated into the aquarium as they also require an appropriate day/night cycle for photosynthesis.

Fluorescent tubes are a common form of aquarium lighting. They are available in a wide range of sizes, wattages and colours, the most popular size being the T8 tube,

2.5cm (1in) in diameter. They are also manufactured in standard lengths, which correspond to a particular wattage.

Conventionally, standard lengths are available in gradients of 15cm (6in). The tube you select should be 15cm (6in) shorter than the length of your aquarium to allow room for the end caps and so that it fits into the hood. Choose, for example, a 75cm (30in) tube for a 90cm (36in) aquarium. Using a reflector behind a fluorescent tube will direct more light into the aquarium.

In more recent years, a narrower and brighter fluorescent tube known as the T5 (derived from its 5/8" width) has become increasingly popular. These tubes provide more lighting power in the same or smaller length tube than standard fluorescents. They are useful for deep tanks, and for those wishing to grow high-maintenance plants.

For a tank which does not contain live plants, select a tube which enhances the colours of the fish, but is not so bright so as to encourage excessive algal growth. Many tubes described as 'warm' or 'warm white' are useful for this purpose. For planted tanks, tubes described as 'bright daylight' or 'midday sun' are particularly suitable. Fluorescent tubes are often rated by their 'colour temperature', measured in degrees Kelvin (K). Most 'bright daylight' tubes have a colour temperature between 5500-7500K. Higher colour temperatures of 10 000-20 000K are normally used in marine aquaria.

In larger tanks, combining two different fluorescent tubes can enhance fish colours and provide a good spectrum for plant growth. Another advantage of using multiple tubes is that you can switch them on and off separately. This can be used to good effect to provide a dusk/dawn effect. You can use blue moonlight or actinic tubes for this purpose.

Metal halide lighting is the ultimate lighting system for very deep tanks, those that are heavily planted or those containing species with highlight requirements. It is referred to as a 'point source' and provides a pleasant dappled effect.

Filtration

A filter is the essential life-support unit of an aquarium. Along with regular water changes, it keeps fish healthy in an artificial environment where they do not have the benefit of the huge volumes of water found in lakes and rivers, and the natural ecosystems that exist there.

A filter performs a number of important functions:

- Mechanical filtration is perhaps the most immediately obvious function. A medium such as sponge/foam or filter wool physically strains large particles from the water. This keeps the water clear and prevents dirt building up excessively in the tank.

- Biological filtration, or biofiltration, is concerned with beneficial bacteria breaking down harmful wastes in the aquarium. Some bacteria and other microorganisms are capable of breaking down more complex waste, but the ones of primary concern to the aquarist are those involved in the nitrogen cycle. These bacteria function most efficiently if they are able to colonize an area with a good flow of oxygenated water bringing their food source to them. Most filter designs have an area intended for bacterial colonization to take place. In simple filters, this may be a sponge, which also filters the water mechanically. In more complex designs, there are specific biomedia that have a high surface area for bacterial growth. Usually this will have a mechanical prefilter to prevent the biomedia from becoming clogged with dirt.

- Chemical filtration, referred to more accurately in some cases as adsorption, refers to the binding of substances to a surface (as opposed to absorption, where the absorbing medium takes the material inside).

The most commonly used adsorption medium is activated carbon, though others are available which bind specific substances such as phosphate.

Left: Different media serve different purposes — filter sponge/foam can act mechanically to strain particles from the water, as well as biologically once mature. Plastic bioballs have an irregular shape that increases the surface area for maximum biofiltration capacity.

Choosing the Correct Filter

A number of factors can influence the choice of a filter. The most obvious are simply:

- The size of the tank. Large tanks require a large pump to circulate the water, and a large filter capacity to handle more waste. Manufacturers of aquarium filters normally give guidelines on the tank-size ratings for each filter. It's always wise to opt for a slightly larger filter to allow for a margin of error.

- The proposed livestock. Fish such as large cichlids and catfish require more filtration than small community fish.

- A heavily planted tank also justifies a different approach to filtration than one that does not contain any live plants, in particular excessive circulation/aeration should be avoided, to prevent the loss of carbon dioxide (see pp33-35).

Choose a filter providing a combination of mechanical, biological and possibly chemical filtration. The ideal solution in some cases may be a combination of two or more different filter types.

You can rate the performance of a filter not only by its pump-circulation rate, but also by its media capacity and type, and the contact time between the media and the water, which is important for efficient biofiltration. An appropriately designed filter with a moderate rate of water flowing through it, using biomedia with a high surface area, allows for maximum contact time.

Right: Canister filters have a large capacity for different filtration media, and are particularly suitable for a larger or heavily-stocked aquarium.

Types of filters

Under-Gravel Filtration

The under-gravel filter, or UGF, was once the mainstay of aquarium filtration, but has declined in popularity with the availability of alternative filtration technologies.

It works by drawing water down through the gravel substrate, which is supported by a grid on the floor of the aquarium. An external air pump produces a rising stream of air bubbles in an uplift tube, circulating the water back to the aquarium surface. (You can use a powerhead instead of an air pump. This is a specific type of water pump that you place on top of an airlift tube.)

The gravel itself functions as a biofiltration medium, and due to the large surface area, works well if you maintain it properly. UGF also keeps the water looking clean because it acts as a mechanical filter drawing suspended particles down into the gravel. However, if excessive debris builds up in the gravel over time it greatly reduces the biofiltration efficiency. A large amount of debris breaking down in the gravel is likely to lead to high nitrate and phosphate levels, and a sinking pH. You should therefore 'vacuum' the gravel regularly during water changes. Contrary to popular myth, vacuuming dirt from the gravel is unlikely to remove a

significant amount of the essential nitrifying bacteria, which attach strongly to surfaces in a 'biofilm'.

You cannot use UGF where there is sand on the floor of the aquarium, as it is too fine and the particles would fall through the supporting grid. It can also prove problematic in aquaria containing fish that like to dig, like many cichlids, because their digging activities short-circuit the gravel bed.

Although it is possible to grow plants in tanks with UGF, UGF is considered less suitable for planted tanks, because it is difficult to 'vacuum' the gravel without damaging plants, and root growth can clog the gravel bed. In addition, the unnatural flow of water past the plant roots affects their nutrient uptake.

A variation on this design, known as Reverse-Flow UGF (RF-UGF), aims to remove the major disadvantage of UGF by mechanically prefiltering the water, to prevent dirt building up in the gravel. A canister filter or a special powerhead is used to prefilter the water before it forces it down and up through the gravel bed.

Using RF-UGF alone results in minimal circulation or surface agitation, and low oxygen problems. It is therefore advisable to use additional aeration/circulation.

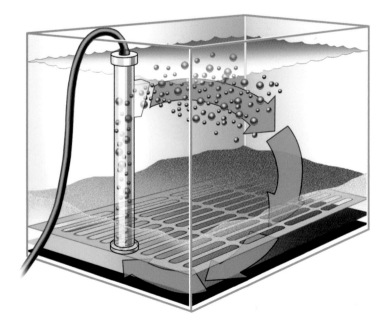

Left: Undergravel filters draw water down through the gravel bed on the floor of the aquarium, which provides a large surface area for biofiltration to take place.

26

Internal Power Filter

Internal power filters are the most popular choice for small to medium tanks, up to around 180l (40 imperial gallons).

With their relatively fast turnover rates, these filters provide good mechanical filtration. Their biomedia capacity is relatively small, but usually sufficient for an average community-tank setup. If the tank is stocked heavily or contains large fish and messy feeders, a second or larger filter may be necessary. A sponge insert usually provides both the mechanical- and biofiltration.

Some newer power-filter designs are modular, or provide extra space to make use of activated carbon, or other specific media. Additional features may include an adjustable output direction, variable flow rate, and an optional venturi attachment that adds air bubbles to the output stream.

You need to clean internal power filters quite regularly, normally every one to two weeks. If more frequent cleaning is required, the tank may be overstocked, or the filter is simply not large enough to cope.

Cleaning is a fairly simple task, and to restore flow usually just involves squeezing out the sponge in aquarium water (to avoid harming the nitrifying bacteria). Some designs incorporate twin sponges, so that thay can be cleaned (or if necessary replaced) alternately, avoiding the loss of the biologically mature media.

In larger tanks, you can use more than one internal filter, or combine it with an external canister filter, which is very effective. In the USA, in particular, many people use HOT/HOB (Hang-On-Tank/Hang-On-Back) power filters. These are similar in many respects to internal power filters, but only the intake and return pipes are inside the aquarium. The media is often cartridge-based so that they are easy to replace. Unfortunately, many earlier designs did not incorporate an area for biofiltration, due to the complete replacement of the media at regular intervals. This shortcoming has been addressed in some new designs.

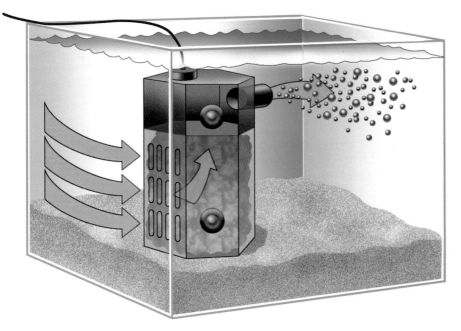

Left: Internal power filters usually draw water through sponge media, which acts as a mechanical and biological filter medium. The water pump creates a stronger flow than air-powered devices.

Décor

As well as enhancing the look of the aquarium, tank décor should provide a secure and preferably natural environment for fish. It is impossible to accurately recreate many natural biotopes in an aquarium, but it is possible to provide appropriate décor, so it is worth finding out a little about the natural environment of the species you wish to keep.

There is a huge range of artificial décor available. It is recommended that you only buy items specifically for use in aquaria, as other items could release paint and varnish into the water, which could prove toxic to fish. The items available vary from sunken shipwrecks and skulls to more natural-looking items like artificial rocks or twisted tree roots. As long as they are safe for the fish, your choice is limited only by personal taste.

Right: Different kinds of background are available for your tank — one of the simplest is 'background on a roll', which is attached to the outside of the tank.

Opposite: Examples of substrate materials; from left to right these are: crushed shell, river sand, crushed coral, coloured gravel and black gravel.

Backgrounds

Fitting a background to a tank will make fish feel more secure, since they will not be exposed on all sides. The choice of background can also make a significant difference to the appearance of an aquarium. As well as complimenting the décor, it hides the wall behind the aquarium and any electrical wiring or tubing which may run behind it.

A common way of providing a background is to fix a background roll to the outside of the tank. This is available in a range of heights to suit different tanks, and in a wide variety of designs. Some background rolls may be

double-sided, so you can occasionally change your background scenery if you wish! Such background pictures may look shiny and artificial to some, but they generally provide a suitable backdrop to the other décor in the tank. There are some designs with a matt finish which have a clever three-dimensional appearance.

Some manufacturers produce textured three-dimensional backgrounds that fit inside the tank. You need to permanently fix these backgrounds in place before filling the tank. Some three-dimensional backgrounds, while expensive, certainly give a dramatic appearance to the aquarium.

Other background options include fixing flat pieces of natural material, such as slate, to the back glass using silicone sealant. Some may opt to paint the back of their tank a permanent plain colour; dark colours such as various shades of blue, dark green or matt black tend to work best.

Substrate

The substrate material you choose for the bottom of the aquarium should be both aesthetic and functional. In some cases, such as quarantine or fry-rearing tanks, it may be preferable to have a bare glass bottom that is easy to clean. For most setups, however, it is best to have gravel or sand on the bottom because it creates a natural environment for the fish and offers the essential bacteria, that break down waste, a large surface area for colonisation.

Some substrate materials may often raise the hardness and pH of aquarium water. This may be undesirable in many setups, unless you are keeping hard-water fish such as African cichlids, in which case you may select the substrate and décor for that reason.

Coral gravel, coral sand and even some standard pea gravels can all harden water. For soft-water setups, sand, fine quartz gravel or other gravels specifically sold as 'inert' are a safer option.

Aquarium substrates are available in a variety of colours and size grades. What you choose is largely the result of personal taste, but natural colours tend to look more satisfactory in most setups than bright, gaudy colours! The size of the substrate is also significant. Large grades of gravel will allow debris to fall down more easily between the gravel. Pea gravel (about 3-5mm in size) is used a lot. Fine grades are useful in planted tanks. All gravel should be smooth to prevent bottom dwelling fish from being hurt.

Fine sand is also an appropriate substrate. Standard aquaria sand, children's play sand and fine horticultural 'silver sand' are all suitable and usually inert. Do not use builders' sand, as it is likely to be impure and may affect water chemistry. Sand is the substrate of choice for many bottom dwelling fish particularly those that like to sift the substrate for food or bury themselves partially in it.

Rocks

You can use rocks to great effect in tank décor: to break up the aquascape into separate territories, form caves and generally enhance the appearance of an aquarium. You can simulate a stony river bed with rounded pebbles, or place them around plant roots, to reduce the chances of fish digging them up. In some setups, rocks may predominate the tank décor, such as in tanks prepared for African Rift Lake cichlids.

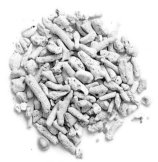

The rock you choose is important. There are many types available, but not all are safe to use in aquaria. Some rocks may harden the water and increase pH, which is undesirable for soft-water fish. (If the tank only contains fish that live in hard water, such as Rift Lake cichlids and livebearers from Central America, this is not a concern and may actually be beneficial to them.) Limestone and other rocks based on calcareous material increase hardness and pH, whereas others such as slate and granite are inert. Very hard forms of limestone may release very little in the way of hardening salts, whereas softer forms, like the crumbly tufa rock, will almost certainly affect pH and hardness. Also, avoid any rocks with obvious silvery metallic veins running through them, as they could release toxic levels of heavy metals into the water.

Note that the more hard and alkaline the water becomes, the less it will leach the rocks of salts. If your tank has hard water to begin with, it will have little effect, even on limestone-based rocks. Soft and acidic water, on the other hand, causes more significant leaching.

Wood

Wood can look very effective when used as part of the tank décor, especially in combination with plants. Various types of bogwood are on sale for aquarium use and you can collect branches to use in your aquarium. This should be dead wood, and you should remove the bark. Suitable woods include beech, birch and ash.

You should presoak any wood you wish to use in an aquarium for a couple of weeks and change the water regularly. This will allow some of the tannins to be leached from the wood, which would otherwise have discoloured the aquarium water. If discolouration does occur, gradually reduce it by changing more water than usual for routine water changes. However, adding activated carbon to the filter will help to remove the tannins more quickly.

Released tannins are not harmful and, in fact, are similar to substances released from peat or found in 'Amazon extracts' which create soft-water conditions. They can, in some situations, lead to an undesirable drop in pH.

Left: Layered rock, smooth stones and hole-filled lava or limestone-based rocks can all be used to break up the aquascape in a suitable setup.
Below: From top to bottom: Bogwood, driftwood and tangled roots can be used to great effect when aquascaping the aquarium.

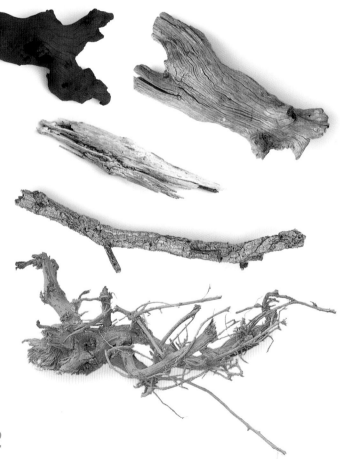

Plants

Some would say that live plants represent the ultimate in aquarium décor. A nicely aquascaped tank has visual appeal and creates a complete ecosystem for fish.

Plants also perform other useful functions in an aquarium: in the daytime they add oxygen to the water and take up ammonia, nitrate and phosphate thereby improving water quality and reducing the growth of algae. Plants can also absorb other potential toxins, such as heavy metals. The following is a selection of commonly available aquarium plants:

Common aquarium plants

Anubias species

Origin: Africa
Lighting: Moderate
Temp: 20-30°C (68-86°F)
Water: Ideally quite soft and acidic, but tolerates harder water.
Notes: Slow growing. Can be attached to bogwood or rocks.

Aponogeton crispus

Origin: Southeast Asia
Lighting: Bright
Temp: 15-32°C (59-90°F)
Water: Not critical, but ideally quite soft and acidic.
Notes: Fast growing and attractive plant.

Ceratopteris thalictroides
Indian Fern

Origin: Southeast Asia
Lighting: Bright
Temp: 20-26°C (68-79°F)
Water: Ideally soft and acidic, but tolerates harder water.
Notes: Can be grown submerged or as a floating plant.

Echinodorus species
Amazon Swords

Origin: South America
Lighting: Moderate to bright
Temp: 15-30°C (59-86°F)
Water: Not critical, but ideally fairly soft and acidic to neutral.
Notes: Many similar species available. Thrives with substrate fertilization.

Echinodorus tenellus
Pygmy Chain Sword

Origin: North and South America

Lighting: Moderate

Temp: 15-26°C (59-79°F)

Water: Not critical.

Notes: Good foreground plant, spreads quickly in ideal conditions.

Hygrophila polysperma
Indian Water Star

Origin: Southeast Asia

Lighting: Bright

Temp: 15-30°C (59-86°F)

Water: Not critical.

Notes: Hardy and easy to grow.

Egeria densa
Giant Elodia, Waterweed

Origin: Central and South America

Lighting: Bright

Temp: 10-25°C (50-77°F)

Water: Not critical, but better in hard and alkaline water.

Notes: Fast growing and low maintenance.

Limnophila sessiloflora
Ambulia

Origin: Southeast Asia

Lighting: Bright

Temp: 22-28°C (72-82°F)

Water: Not critical.

Notes: Very fast growing and undemanding.

Hygrophila difformis
Water Wisteria

Origin: Southeast Asia

Lighting: Bright

Temp: 20-30°C (68-86°F)

Water: Not critical, fairly soft and slightly acidic water ideal.

Notes: Fast growing and low maintenance, but often eaten by herbivorous fish.

Ludwigia repens

Origin: North America

Lighting: Bright

Temp: 15-26°C (59-79°F)

Water: Not critical.

Notes: Fast growing and low maintenance.

Microsorium pteropus
Java Fern

Origin: Southeast Asia

Lighting: Low to Moderate

Temp: 20-25°C (68-77°F)

Water: Not critical,

low maintenance.

Notes: Very hardy. Should be

attached to bogwood or rocks.

Vallisneria tortifolia
Twisted Vallis

Origin: Widespread in tropical

and subtropical areas.

Lighting: Bright

Temp: 15-30°C (59-86°F)

Water: Not critical, does well in

hard water.

Notes: Low maintenance. Good

background plant.

Nymphaea lotus
Tiger Lily

Origin: Africa

Lighting: Bright

Temp: 22-30°C (72-86°F)

Water: Not critical.

Notes: Sends stems to the

surface. Very attractive

specimen plant.

Vesicularia dubyana
Java Moss

Origin: Southeast Asia

Lighting: Low to Moderate

Temp: 20-26°C (68-79°F)

Water: pH and hardness

not critical.

Notes: Should attach to

bogwood or rocks, where it

will spread over the surface.

Vallisneria spiralis
Straight Vallis

Origin: Widespread in tropical

and subtropical areas.

Lighting: Bright

Temp: 15-30°C (59-86°F)

Water: Not critical, does well in

harder water.

Notes: Undemanding. Good

background plant.

Maintenance & Health

The old saying: 'Prevention is better than cure' is especially true of aquarium fish and their health. If you take the time to learn about the needs of your fish and how to care for them properly, you will hopefully encounter disease only on rare occasions.

Disease organisms are always present in the aquarium, but they do not normally affect healthy fish. They take hold when fish are injured, weak or stressed due to poor water quality, the aggression of other fish, or as a result of handling and transportation.

The first step in preventing disease is to provide stable, good quality water, maintain your aquarium at a specific, constant temperature and to feed your fish appropriately. Nevertheless, even when you practise good tank mainte-nance, there may unfortunately be occasions when there is a disease outbreak. Fortunately, you can cure many common fish diseases, particularly if you notice them early. For this reason, you should observe your fish closely and note any changes in their behaviour or appearance. Some diseases have fairly obvious and specific symptoms (see pp 39-41). General early warning signs to look out for include a loss of appetite, body colours appearing darker or paler than nor-mal, rapid gill movement and scratching against décor.

Water Changes

Regular partial water changes are perhaps the single most important thing you can do to keep your fish healthy. In an aquarium, waste such as nitrate can build up quickly and have negative effects on the health and vitality of your fish.

Stick to a regular schedule for water changes and never leave them until the tank looks dirty or the fish seem unwell. Changing about 25% of the volume of the tank water every two weeks is a sensible minimum. Do not leave it for as long as a month — it is better to change small volumes of water more frequently, rather than change a very large volume less often.

Some species or tank setups require a weekly 20-25% water change, which minimizes changes in the water chem-istry and reduces the stress on fish. These setups include:

- Heavily-stocked tanks that are near to their maximum limit of fish.
- Small tanks where the small volume of water means waste levels are able to rise more quickly, and the tank is inherently less stable.
- Tanks containing large fish, particularly messy feeders such as large cichlids and predatory fish that eat a lot of high-protein foods.

Tanks for breeding and raising fry. Improved growth rates are reported where frequent water changes have been carried out.

Get into the habit of checking regularly for nitrates as the nitrate level in a tank is a useful indicator of whether your water-change schedule is sufficient. It is best to maintain a nitrate level below 50mg/l (=ppm) – below 25mg/l is even better. If the nitrate level is significantly above 50mg/l, you may need to increase your water changes. (It is possible to use specific resins or anaerobic filter systems to reduce nitrate levels.)

When doing water changes, siphon as much dirt and debris from the substrate as possible. This prevents their decomposition, which adds to the waste levels of nitrate and phosphate.

If you use gravel, suck up the dirt regularly using a gravel siphon pushed into the substrate. Sand can be cleaned by holding a piece of plain siphon hose just above the surface of the sand. With a little practice it becomes easy to suck away debris (which mostly stays on the surface) without also sucking up the sand grains to any significant degree.

Feeding

Fish require the correct diet if they are to thrive. Some fish are omnivorous. Other fish may be more specialized feeders. Herbivores consume mainly vegetable matter, and may suffer if you constantly feed them high-protein foods. Likewise, some fish are primarily carnivores and only eat meaty foods.

A wide range of commercial foods are available these days, which along with a few household vegetables and frozen or live foods, cater for the required dietary requirements of most fish kept in aquaria.

Dry aquarium foods such as flakes, pellets and granular foods make an excellent staple diet for many fish. Research into the nutritional needs of fish has led to the production of balanced foods that contain a guaranteed vitamin and protein component. Not all fish will eat dry aquarium foods, and some species may require frozen or live foods. Frozen, freeze-dried and live foods also add variety to the diet, and are used to bring fish into breeding condition.

Right: Dried foods such as flakes, pellets and sticks can provide part of the staple diet of many fish.

Opposite: Providing good water quality and an appropriate setup with the correct combination of fish will go a long way towards preventing problems in the aquarium.

How Much Food, and How Often?

For many common community fish, a small feeding one to two times a day is sufficient. Feed young fry small amounts several times a day and adult fish once a day. It is beneficial to skip a day of feeding every week or two.

Feed grazers such as algae eaters and other herbivores continually. In some cases, natural algal growth in the tank may provide for this. You do not need to feed large carnivorous and predatory fishes as often. Juvenile fish, on the other hand, need food once a day and, as the fish grows, reduce feedings to every other day. Adult predatory fish may need to eat only once or twice a week as it is very easy for them to overindulge, which in the longterm is likely to cause health problems and to reduce their lifespan.

In a natural environment, fish have to work hard to find food which may be scarce at times – a sharp contrast to an aquarium where food is often available in excess on a daily basis. It is tempting to feed fish whenever they 'look hungry', which is probably most of the time! Healthy fish almost never refuse a suitable food, so if there is excess food left on the floor of the aquarium, then it is likely that you are overfeeding. (An exception to this would be slow-dissolving tablet food or household vegetables for bottom feeding or herbivorous fish.)

Overfeeding can also affect the water quality of tanks, especially in tanks that are newly set up, overstocked, have inadequate filtration systems or that have few partial water changes. One of the most serious consequences of overfeeding, particularly in immature tanks, is a rise in ammonia or nitrite levels. In mature tanks that have been running for some time, high nitrate levels and a sinking pH are often a problem (see pp16-18).

Overfeeding can also reduce the lifespan of fish, particularly in cases where owners feed carnivorous fish mammal meat such as beef heart, which leads to fatty deposits accumulating around organs such as the liver.

Left: Malawi cichlids are hardy fish that rarely suffer from disease. The rock-dwelling 'mbuna' are the most commonly kept and should be provided with a larger proportion of vegetable matter in their diet.

As fish do not have a regular food supply in the wild, it does them no harm to be without food for a few days, or even a week or more, if you are away on vacation. If you are unable to feed your fish for a longer period, other options are available. Feeder blocks slowly dissolve in the water to release food. Use these with caution, however, and test them in advance. You may be able to get a friend or relative to feed your fish while you are away. It may be useful to prepare the correct daily portions in advance in small sealed bags with the correct day written on them — this way there should be little chance of accidental overfeeding. Auto-feeders, which deliver food at pre-set intervals, are also available.

Diseases

It is not possible to cover the complete spectrum of the diagnosis and treatment of fish diseases in this chapter. However, most disease outbreaks in the aquarium are due to a small number of common infections, which are listed here.

Bacterial Diseases

Bacterial diseases can take a number of forms. They may be external, causing symptoms such as fin erosion (*Finrot*), cloudy eyes, general sores and mouth erosion (*Columnaris*).

You can usually treat these external infections successfully if you catch them early. Commercial anti-bacterial medication can be purchased at any aquatic store, but antibiotics require a veterinary prescription in many countries, though they can be purchased over the counter in the USA.

Bacterial infections can also be internal. A condition known as *Dropsy* is a common symptom of internal bacterial disease, although there are other possible causes. The main symptom of *dropsy* is a swollen body, accompanied by scales sticking out which causes a 'pine-cone' appearance. Often, it is much more difficult to treat internal bacterial diseases, especially if the symptoms are advanced.

Fungal Infections

Fungal infections are almost always secondary infections, that is, they occur after another infectious agent has caused primary damage, or following physical damage. Fish may succumb to fungal infections after hurting themselves on sharp aquarium décor, after rough handling during netting, or following a primary infection of parasites or bacteria.

Fungus does not generally appear on healthy tissue, and should not spread to other healthy fish. A fungal infection appears as fluffy, cottonwool-like growths. Some bacterial infections can appear similar to fungus, because they manifest themselves as grey-white threads.

Many forms of commercial medication treat both bacterial and fungal infections, providing a safeguard in the event of misdiagnoses. Isolate infected fish where possible, and treat with an antifungal medication according to the manufacturer's instructions.

Protozoan-type Parasite Diseases

Parasite diseases are often highly contagious within the confines of an aquarium. The most common parasite diseases are Whitespot (Ich or *Ichthyophthirius*) – which appears on the fins as white spots, the size of salt grains – but later spreads to the whole body. Velvet

Above: Anchor-worm, whitespot, striped fish lice.

(*Piscinoodinium*) appears as tiny grey-white 'dust' spots, and the so-called 'Slime diseases' (*Costia/Ichthyobodo, Chilodonella, Trichodina*) appear as white-grey film.

The parasites also irritate the fish which may, in turn, scratch their bodies against décor. They may also clamp their fins and move their gills quickly. You can treat all of these infections with commercial antiparasite medication.

Large parasites such as Anchor Worms (*Lernaeidae* family) and Fish Lice (*Argulus*) are less common in tropical aquarium fish, but are seen occasionally on wild-caught fish.

Viral Diseases

Relatively little is known about viral diseases in aquarium fish. It is possible that viruses may be responsible for mystery deaths where no environmental problems or disease symptoms are apparent. It is also likely that a number of viral diseases may restrict themselves to single species or closely related species.

Medication

When using any medication, be sure to follow the instructions exactly. In general, you should never use more than one medication at a time, unless it is specifically indicated that it is safe to do so.

Where a specific fish has succumbed to disease, it may be preferable to treat it in a hospital/isolation tank. It may, however, also be necessary to treat the main tank. This is particularly true of parasite diseases such as Whitespot (Ich), which has a number of lifecycle stages.

Always complete the course of medication, even if the symptoms have disappeared. An incomplete course may not eliminate the infection entirely, and could establish medication-resistant strains of disease organisms.

Table of disease symptoms

The table below outlines some of the signs and symptoms observed in some of the more commonly encountered fish ailments.

- ■ definite sign of disease
- ▨ possible sign of disease

Symptoms	Finrot	Whitespot	Velvet	Slime diseases	Columnaris	Fungus	Large parasites eg. flukes	Dropsy	Internal parasitic worms
Frayed fins	■				▨				
Cottonwool-like growths						■			
Mouth eroded					■				
Ulcerated body					■		▨	▨	
White 'salt-grain' spots		■							
Fine dusting of tiny spots			■						
Grey-white slime on body				■	■				
Clamped fins		■							
Rapid gill movement		▨	■				▨		
Scratching against décor		■	■	■			■		
Swollen body								■	▨
Scales sticking out								■	
Emaciated			▨						■
Curvature of spine									■

Setting Up

You should set up your tank at least a few days before buying any fish. This allows time for the water to stabilize and for you to check that all the equipment is working properly.

When you are happy with the layout of your tank, you can begin to add water. This is likely to be easier with a hosepipe than with buckets, but in either case, try to add water gently by directing it onto a rock, or a dish put in the tank. This will prevent you from stirring up the substrate. Remember always to dechlorinate fresh tap water before using it.

There is no point however, in waiting much longer than a week before adding the fish, as the tank will not begin to mature properly without them or an alternative source of ammonia (see pp25, 36, 38).

Above: Aquascaping the tank is one of the fun parts of setting up an aquarium and provides plenty of scope to use your creative abilities.

1

Ensure that the tank is standing on a firm, flat surface. Add a background to the tank to make the fish feel more secure.

2

Wash the gravel or sand for the bottom of the tank. Here gravel is being added on top of an under-gravel filter plate.

3

Add rocks, wood and any other décor as required. Ensure that all rocks are placed securely so that they cannot fall.

4

Add water with a hose, or by pouring it slowly onto a plate or similar to avoid stirring up the substrate.

Suggestions for Tank Setups

As a starting point, here are a few suggestions to inspire you to create a themed or biotope tank representing a particular natural habitat.

Equatorial river

Above: An Amazon riverbank, Brazil.

Habitat: Amazonian 'Blackwater'.

Décor: Sandy substrate, several large pieces of bogwood and a few small twigs or branches. No plants.

Water parameters:
Temperature: 24-26°C (75-79°F)
pH: 6.0-6.9
Hardness: GH 1-3°, KH 2-3°

Suggested tank size: Minimum 120 x 46 x 46cm (48 x 18 x 18in)

Filtration: External canister filter.

Water changes: 25% every week.

Feeding: Flake and granular food; various live and frozen foods. Veggie-based flakes for Silver Dollars, as well as household vegetables. Include sinking algal wafers to supplement the diet of Catfish (*Loricarids*). Feed one to two times a day.

Suggested Fish Stock:

6 *Metynnis hypsauchen* or *Mefynnis argenteus* (Silver Dollars)
2 *Geophagus brasiliensis* (Pearl Cichlid)
4 *Pimellodus pictus* (Pictus Catfish)
2-3 *Loricarids* (Suckermouth Catfish)

Notes: The weekly water changes will help prevent a pH crash with low KH levels. I have chosen large fish in this example, but Tetras and Corydoras catfish could be used for a small tank.

The bogwood will leach tannins and simulate the dark tea-coloured appearance of Amazonian blackwater. You could use a commercial blackwater 'tonic' or filter your aquarium water through peat.

River rapids

Habitat: Fast-flowing river, where shallow water flows rapidly over a stony bottom, with a few pieces of wood caught between rocks and some plants hanging onto the rocks despite the strong current. This could be given a South American, Asian or African theme.

Décor: Rounded stones, a few pieces of driftwood, a few plants such as *Anubias* attached to rocks or wood.

Water parameters:
Temperature: 24-26°C (75-79°F)
pH: 6.5-7.5
Hardness: GH 5-10°, KH 3-6°. Highly oxygenated.

Suggested tank size: Minimum 150 x 38 x 46cm (60 x 15 x 18in)

Filtration: Internal power filter.

Water changes: 25% every week.

Feeding: Flake and granular food, various live and frozen food. Feed one to two times a day.

Above: Shallow river rapids.

Suggested Fish Stock:
For an African theme:
Small group of:
Steatocranus tinanti (African River Cichlid)
Teleogramma brichardi
Synodontis brichardi catfish

Notes: You could use two power filters at either end of the tank to provide strong water movement.

Tropical lake 1

Habitat: Rocky shores of Lake Malawi in Rift Valley, East Africa, home to the *mbuna* (Malawi rockfish).

Décor: An abundance of rocks covering the back and sides of the aquarium, with open swimming space in front. Arrange the rocks to form many open caves with an entry and exit to allow harassed fish to escape.

Water parameters:
Temperature: 24-26°C (75-79°F)
pH: 7.5-8.5
Hardness: GH 7°+, KH 10°+. Well oxygenated.

Suggested tank size: Minimum 120 x 38 x 46cm (48 x 15 x 18in)

Filtration: External canister and internal power filter.

Water changes: 25-30% per week.

Feeding: Spirulina/veggie flakes; green pellets; mysis; brine shrimp; daphnia. Feed twice a day. Avoid high-protein meaty foods.

Suggested Fish Stock: Ideally, stock three to five of each species, one male and two to four females
In tanks up to 120cm (48in):
Iodotropheus sprengerae (Rusty cichlid)
Labidochromis caeruleus (Yellow Lab/Canary cichlid)
Labidochromis flavigulus
Pseudotropheus acei
Pseudotropheus saulosi
Pseudotropheus socolofi (Powder Blue cichlid)

Above: Rocky lake shoreline.

In tanks 120cm (48in) and more:
Cynotilapia afra
Labeotropheus trewavassae (Trewavas' cichlid)
Labidochromis sp. "Hongi"
Melanochromis johanni
Metriaclima estherae (Red Zebra)
Pseudotropheus demasoni (Demason's Cichlid)
Pseudotropheus elongatus

Tropical lake 2

Habitat: Rocky shores and open sandy areas of Lake Tanganyika in the Rift Valley of East Africa.

Décor: Large smooth rocks or pieces of slate, arranged in separate piles to create separate territory areas. Sand substrate with scattered shells.

Water parameters:
Temperature: 25-26°C (77-79°F)
PH: 7.8-9.0

Hardness: GH 10° +, KH 12° +; well oxygenated.

Suggested tank size: Minimum 120 x 38 x 46cm (48 x 15 x 18"); taller tank 46-60cm (18-24") to include *Cyprichromis*.

Filtration: External canister and internal power filter.

Water changes: 20% per week.

Feeding: Flake and granular foods; small cichlid pellets; bloodworm; mysis; brine shrimp; daphnia; mosquito larvae. Feed one to two times a day.

Suggested Fish Stock:
1 pair medium-sized *Neolamprogus* e.g. *N. brichardi*
1 pair *Julidochromis* species
Approximately six shelldwellers e.g. *N. ocellatus*
Trio of *Synodontis petricola* catfish

Above: Large lakes are like inland seas, with waves lapping the beach areas.

In a tall tank:
shoal of *Cyprichromis leptosoma*, numbering six to 12. Depending on tank size, there should be approximately three females per male.
You could swap the *Julidochromis* for one of the slim *Neolamprologus* species such as *N. leleupi* or *N. cylindricus*. As these species are more predatory, the shelldwellers should not be too small.

Notes: Lake Tanganyika is a massive body of water 676km (420 miles) long, and the second deepest lake in the world. It is therefore very stable. You should aim to keep the aquarium parameters stable and the water quality very high.

Planted aquarium

Habitat: Not a specific natural habitat, but it could be themed as Southeast Asian or South American.

Décor: Select live plants and two or three pieces of bogwood to arrange the plants around. Nutrient substrate. Bright lighting.
For an Asian theme: *Hygrophila, Limnophila, Vallisneria* and *Crytocorynes* for the foreground.
For a South American theme: *Echinodorous* (Amazon Swords), with *Echinodoras tenellus* (Pygmy Chain Sword) in the foreground. Floating *Limnobium laevigatum* (Amazon Frogbit).

Water parameters:
Temperature: 24-26°C (75-79°F)
pH: 6.5-7.2
Hardness: GH 4-8°, KH 3-5°
Possibly CO_2 addition.

Suggested tank size: Minimum 120 x 38 x 46cm (48 x 12 x 18in)

Filtration: External canister filter.

Water changes: 20% every one to two weeks.

Feeding: Flake and granular foods, various live and frozen food. Vegetable component. Feed one to two times a day.

Above: Slow-moving water with submerged vegetation.

Suggested Fish Stock:
Southeast Asian theme:
6 *Puntius nigrofasciatus* (Black Ruby Barb)
8 *Danio albolineatus* (Pearl Danio)
4 *Botia striata* (Zebra/Candy-Stripe Loach)
5 *Crossocheilus siamensis* (Siamese Algae Eater)

South American theme:
10 *Hemigrammus bleheri* (Rummy-Nosed Tetra)
6 *Hyphessobrycon sweglesi* (Red Phantom Tetra)
2 *Microgeophagus ramerezi* (Ram Cichlids)
6 *Corydoras* catfish
6 *Otocinclus vittatus* (Dwarf Suckermouth catfish)

Notes: Adding CO_2 to water is not vital, but will boost plant growth and create a slightly acidic to neutral pH.

Brackish mangrove swamp

Habitat: The area where freshwater meets the sea, dominated by mangrove trees.

Décor: Roots or tree branches arranged to look like the roots of mangrove trees growing down into the water.

Water parameters:
Temperature: 24-28°C (75-82°F)
PH: 7.0-9.0
Salinity: specific gravity (SG) of 1.005; for the larger tank below, up to 1.015 as the fish mature.
Hardness: Very high due to marine salt; well oxygenated.

Suggested tank size: Minimum 120 x 46 x 46cm (48 x 18 x 18"); large tank to include Scats/Monos – 180 x 46 x 60cm (72 x 18 x 24")

Filtration: Large external canister and internal power filter.

Water changes: 30% every one to two weeks.

Feeding: Flake and granular foods; insects including crickets, bloodworm, mysis, brine shrimp and mosquito larvae. If you've included Scats (*Scatophagus argus*) and Monos (*Monodactylus argenteus* or *Monodactylus sebae*) to your tank add plenty of green foods. Feed one to two times a day.

Above: Typical mangrove habitat.

Suggested Fish Stock:
Group of 4–5 *Toxotes jaculatrix* (Archerfish)
Pair of *Stigmatobius sadanundio* (Knight Gobies)
Trio of *Tetraodon biocellatus* (Figure-8 Puffers)
In a larger tank you could include adult Archerfish instead of the fish mentioned above and:
5–6 *Scatophagus argus* (Scats)
5–6 Monos (*Monodactylus argenteus* or *Monodactylus sebae*)
Trio of *Tetraodon fluviatilis* (Green Puffers)
Trio of *Hexanomatichthys* (Arius) *seemanni* (Shark Catfish)

Notes: Make water brackish using a good quality marine salt mix. You must predissolve this before adding it to the aquarium during water changes.

Tropical Fish

Species Guide

Red Devil
Agassizi's Dwarf Cichlid
Cockatoo Dwarf Cichlid
Oscar
Keyhole Cichlid
Convict Cichlid
Pearl Cichlid
Banded Cichlid
Rainbow Cichlid
Flag Cichlid
Ram
Jack Dempsey
Salvin's Cichlid
Jaguar Cichlid
Angelfish
Discus
Firemouth
Uaru
Black Belt Cichlid

Cyprinids 114–129
Zebra Loach
Clown Loach
Kuhli Loach
Chain Loach
Silver Shark
Tinfoil Barb
Siamese Algae Eater
Red-fin Silver Shark
Pearl Danio
Zebra Danio
Red-tailed Black Shark
Red-finned Shark

Flying Fox
Cigar Shark
Rosy Barb
Red-line Torpedo Barb
Clown Barb
Spanner Barb
Black Ruby Barb
Pentazona Barb
Tiger Barb
Ticto Barb
Cherry Barb
Pygmy Rasbora
Red Scissortail
Scissortail
Harlequin Rasbora
Algae Eater

Killifish 130–131
Steel-blue Killifish
Red-tail Notho

Livebearers 132–135
Four-eyed Fish
Celebes Halfbeak
Molly
Guppy
Swordtail
Platy

Rainbowfish 136–139
Madagascan Rainbow
Red Rainbow
Threadfin Rainbow

Boeseman's Rainbow
Neon dwarf Rainbow
Banded Rainbow

Miscellaneous 140–153
Black Ghost Knife Fish
Siamese Tigerfish
Silver Tigerfish
Knight Goby
Fire Eel
Banded Spiny Eel
Mono
Elephantnose
Clown Knife Fish
Silver Arowana
Asian Arowana
African Butterflyfish
Reedfish
Ornate Bichir
Ocellated Stingray
African Lungfish
Scat
Dwarf Puffer
South American puffer
Figure-8 puffer
Green Puffer
Nile puffer
Giant Puffer
Green-spotted Puffer
Archerfish

Anabantids

The Anabantids, or 'Labyrinth Fish' as they are often known, all share a common feature known as the Labyrinth Organ. This allows them to breathe atmospheric air from the surface of the water, a useful adaptation for surviving in low-oxygen environments.

Most of the Labyrinth fish available to the hobby come from Asia, and a few from Africa. The group most familiar to fishkeepers is probably the Gouramies. Most of these fish share a distinctive shape with long 'feelers' evolved from extended pelvic fins. The Gouramies vary in size from small and somewhat delicate species, to real giants that require a huge aquarium.

Also within the Gourami family are the species of the genus Betta. Although many species are available, by far the most popular and commonly encountered is the Siamese Fighting Fish, Betta splendens; which unfortunately is often sold, and worse, maintained in small, unfiltered containers.

Less familiar Labyrinth Fish, at least to those keeping community fish, are the Snakeheads. These fish are predatory, often aggressive and some species grow very large. This is not true of all species however, and some make excellent aquarium fish for the enthusiast.

ANABANTIDAE (Climbing Gouramies)
Ctenopoma acutirostre
LEOPARD BUSHFISH, SPOTTED CLIMBING PERCH

20cm
8˝

23-28°C
73-82°F

90cm
36˝

Origin: Africa – Congo basin

Tank Setup: Ideally a planted tank with some tall stem plants and pieces of bogwood. The lighting should not be too bright, and you can use floating plants to provide shade. Moderate water movement.

Compatibility/Aquarium Behaviour: Predatory; will eat small fish. Territorial with their own kind. May be timid with larger or more aggressive fish.

Water Chemistry: Fairly soft, slightly acidic to around neutral (pH 6.0-7.5)

Feeding: Carnivorous; feed meaty, frozen or live foods, may eat flakes and pellets.

Sexing: Males have spines on their bodies.

Breeding: Bubblenest builder. Requires very soft and acidic water. Little brood care occurs. An increase in water temperature may trigger spawning.

CHANNIDAE
Channa bleheri
RAINBOW SNAKEHEAD

15cm
6˝

24°C
75°F

90cm
36˝

Origin: Asia – India

Tank Setup: Preferably a well-planted tank with gentle water flow. Make sure the tank has a tight-fitting cover, as these fish are accomplished escape artists!

Compatibility/Aquarium Behaviour: A relatively peaceful species, which is only territorial towards its own kind or very similar-looking fish. However, it must not be kept with smaller community fish.

Water Chemistry: Not critical as long as you avoid extremes.

Feeding: Frozen, live or meaty foods – this species does not eat dry food.

Sexing: No obvious differences

Breeding: Rare in aquaria. Temperatures at the upper end of the tropical range are required. Both parents guard the fry.

HELOSTOMATIDAE (Kissing Gouramies)
Helostoma temminkii
KISSING GOURAMI

15cm
6˝

22-30°C
72-86°F

120cm
48˝

Origin: Southeast Asia – Thailand and Indonesia

Tank Setup: A large tank with robust plants, plenty of open swimming space and a gentle water flow.

Compatibility/Aquarium Behaviour: You can keep this species in a large community tank, but it can be territorial, particularly with other gouramies.

Water Chemistry: Not critical: fairly soft to very hard; pH 6.5-8.5

Feeding: This species is omnivorous, and accepts most foods, which should include some vegetable matter.

Sexing: The sexes are essentially impossible to distinguish.

Breeding: The species requires a temperature at the higher end of the range to breed. It may build a bubblenest; there is no brood care. Eggs hatch in approximately 24 hours.

OSPHRONEMIDAE (Gouramies)
Betta splendens
BETTA/SIAMESE FIGHTING FISH

7cm
3˝

24-29°C
75-84°F

75cm
30˝

Origin: Southeast Asia – Cambodia, Thailand

Minimum Recommended Tank Size: 30cm (12in) for a single male.

Tank Setup: A peaceful planted tank with some floating plants, and gentle water circulation.

Compatibility/Aquarium Behaviour: Usually peaceful, although individuals vary. You should only keep one male per tank. Avoid mixing with fin-nippers that target its elongated finnage.

Water Chemistry: Not critical: fairly soft to medium hard, pH 6.0-8.0

Feeding: Carnivorous; feed small live, as well as frozen and granular foods.

Sexing: Males have elongated finnage.

Breeding: Bubblenest builder; the male will entice the female under the nest. Remove female after spawning. The male will guard the eggs, which should hatch in 24 hours. Feed the fry very fine foods such as baby brine shrimp.

OSPHRONEMIDAE (Gouramies)
Colisa lalia
DWARF GOURAMI

6cm
2″

22-28°C
72-82°

60cm
24″

Origin: India

Tank Setup: A well-planted tank with gentle circulation and some floating plants.

Compatibility/Aquarium Behaviour: This species is usually peaceful, but can become territorial with other gouramies or similar fish, especially when breeding. Best to keep in pairs.

Water Chemistry: Good water quality; soft to medium hard; pH 6.5-7.5

Feeding: Omnivorous; accepts most food. Eagerly takes small frozen and live food; include some vegetable matter in the diet.

Sexing: Males are generally larger and more colourful than the females who tend to be silver.

Breeding: Bubblenest builder. Remove female after spawning. The male guards the eggs and fry; remove free-swimming fry.

OSPHRONEMIDAE (Gouramies)
Macropodus opercularis
PARADISE FISH

10cm
4″

16-27°C
61-80°F

60cm
24″

Origin: Eastern Asia

Tank Setup: Fairly large tank, with refuge for females and gentle circulation.

Compatibility/Aquarium Behaviour: You can keep these fish in a community tank, but males may be aggressive. Keep only one male per tank.

Water Chemistry: Not critical; fairly soft to hard; pH 6.0-8.0

Feeding: Omnivorous; feed flakes and granular foods and supplement with frozen and live food.

Sexing: Males have brighter colours and much longer fins than females.

Breeding: Bubblenest builder. Eggs hatch in about a day and the male usually guards the fry.

55

OSPHRONEMIDAE (Gouramies)
Osphronemus goramy
GIANT GOURAMI

| 70cm | 20-30°C | 180cm |
| 28″ | 68-86°F | 72″ |

Origin: Southeast Asia

Tank Set-up: A very large tank, with a minimum amount of robust décor.

Compatibility/Aquarium Behaviour: Juveniles are quite territorial, but usually mature into 'gentle giants' that can be combined with other large fish in a suitably huge aquarium.

Water Chemistry: Not critical; soft to medium hard; pH 6.2-7.8

Feeding: Omnivorous; accepts almost any food – large pellet foods are ideal as a staple diet; include some green food.

Sexing: Males have more pointed dorsal and anal fins than the females.

Breeding: Reported to build bubblenests using plant material. Eggs take about two days to hatch. The male will guard the eggs and fry.

OSPHRONEMIDAE (Gouramies)
Trichogaster leeri
PEARL GOURAMI, LACE GOURAMI, MOSAIC GOURAMI

| 12,5cm | 23-28°C | 90cm |
| 5″ | 73-82°F | 36″ |

Origin: Southeast Asia – Malaysia, Thailand, Borneo, Sumatra

Tank Setup: Planted tank with gentle circulation and quite a few floating plants.

Compatibility/Aquarium Behaviour: Usually relatively peaceful, but can be territorial with other gouramies or similar fish.

Water Chemistry: Not critical: soft to medium hard; pH 6.5-8.0

Feeding: Omnivorous; accepts most aquarium food.

Sexing: Males have a pointed dorsal fin and extended fin rays on the anal fin and, to a lesser extent, on the dorsal fin. Males show more red on their undersides when breeding.

Breeding: A bubblenest builder. The male will guard the nest and fry. Pairs may become aggressive towards tank mates when spawning.

OSPHRONEMIDAE (Gouramies)

Trichogaster microlepis
MOONLIGHT GOURAMI

15cm
6″

25-29°C
77-84°F

90cm
36″

Origin: Southeast Asia — Cambodia, Malaysia, Singapore, Thailand

Tank Set-up: Planted tank with very gentle circulation and some floating plants

Compatibility/Aquarium Behaviour: Generally a very peaceful species, but may show territorial behaviour towards other gouramies.

Water Chemistry: Not critical: soft to medium hard; pH 6.2-7.8

Feeding: Omnivorous; accepts most foods; include some vegetable matter in the diet.

Sexing: The pelvic fins of males may show orange-red, those of females yellow.

Breeding: Bubblenest builder. The male will care for the fry for the first few days.

OSPHRONEMIDAE (Gouramies)

Trichogaster trichopterus
BLUE GOURAMI, THREE-SPOT GOURAMI

15cm
6″

22-28°C
72-82°F

90cm
36″

Origin: Southeast Asia

Tank Setup: Planted tank with gentle circulation and some floating plants.

Compatibility/Aquarium Behaviour: Can be territorial with other gouramies, and sometimes also with other tank mates. Some individuals (often large males) can become persistently aggressive.

Water Chemistry: Not critical for this hardy fish: soft to medium hard; pH 6.0-8.5

Feeding: Omnivorous; accepts almost any aquarium food.

Sexing: Males have pointed dorsal fins.

Breeding: A bubblenest builder, pairs will become aggressive towards tank mates when spawning. One of the easier gouramies to breed. Remove female after spawning; the male will guard the bubblenest and fry.

Catfish

The catfish comprise a large order of fish (an 'order' is the scientific term for the next classification level above families, and usually contains several families within it). Catfish belong to the order Siluriformes, which contains more than 30 families and over 2500 species. Although many catfish share certain common features, there is enormous diversity in their size and shape.

One common feature among catfish is that they are scaleless. Some have 'armour' consisting of bony plates instead, and many employ fin spines as a means of defence. Catfish also have barbels (or 'whiskers', hence the common name).

Catfish are hugely popular as aquarium fish, and their diversity means that there is a catfish to suit almost every aquarium. They are often sought as scroungers and scavengers for the aquarium, sometimes in the mistaken belief that this will reduce the need for maintenance by the fishkeeper! Though many catfish are well adapted for scavenging food, they require a good diet to thrive.

The peaceful Corydoras catfish are very popular bottomfeeders for community aquaria, while many 'suckermouth' catfish are purchased to help reduce algae in the aquarium, though not all species actually include algae in their diet. Many catfish are predatory, particularly those with long barbels, and are not generally suitable for community tanks.

ARIIDAE (Sea catfish)

Hexanematichthys seemanni

COLOMBIAN SHARK CATFISH, TETE SEA CATFISH

35cm 14″ 21-26°C 70-79°F 180cm 72″

Size: Usually approximately 30-35cm (12-14in), but can grow larger.

Origin: North, Central and South American rivers and estuaries

Tank Setup: A large brackish tank with smooth rocks or well-soaked bogwood for décor and plenty of open swimming space in the lower levels.

Compatibility/Aquarium Behaviour: Highly predatory; do not keep with small fish. Best kept with large shoaling brackish fish, such as adult scats or monos.

Water Chemistry: Neutral to alkaline pH; slightly brackish to full marine conditions.

Feeding: Carnivorous; feed meaty, frozen or live food such as bloodworm for juveniles and pieces of mussel, prawn or shrimp for adults. They will also take sinking pellet food, which can vary the diet.

Sexing: Males are more slender than females.

Breeding: Rarely spawned in captivity; tank water requires a change in salinity.

ASPREDINIDAE (Banjo catfish)

Bunocephalus coracoideus

BANJO CATFISH

12,5cm 5″ 23-28°C 73-82°F 75cm 30″

Origin: South America – Amazon River basin

Tank Setup: A soft substrate, preferably sand, with bogwood for décor, and live plants if desired. Subdued lighting.

Compatibility/Aquarium Behaviour: A shy and secretive species which is not aggressive towards other fish.

Water Chemistry: Not critical, but fairly soft water, neutral to slightly acidic, would be ideal.

Feeding: Primarily an insectivore; feed frozen or live foods; will usually take sinking pellet and granular food.

Sexing: Females are larger and deeper bodied than males.

Breeding: Group spawning occurs at night, with a scattering of a large number of eggs.

AUCHENIPTERIDAE (Driftwood catfish)
Tatia perugiae
PERUGIA'S WOODCAT

5cm
2″

23-28°C
73-82°F

60cm
24″

Origin: South America – Upper Amazon River basin

Tank Setup: Provide small caves using bogwood or rocks, and a sand or fine gravel substrate.

Compatibility/Aquarium Behaviour: A peaceful species that is quite secretive and more active at night.

Water Chemistry: Soft to slightly hard, and slightly acidic.

Feeding: Insectivorous; feed small frozen and live food.

Sexing: Males have a modified anal fin on a short stalk.

Breeding: Aquarium spawnings are becoming more common. Internal fertilization takes place, with the female depositing the eggs 24-48 hours later. She will guard the eggs.

BAGRIDAE (Bagrid catfish)
Hemibagrus wyckii
CRYSTAL-EYED CATFISH

70cm
28″

22-25°C
72-77°F

180cm
72″

Origin: Asia – Thailand to Indonesia

Tank Setup: Minimal décor, with plenty of open space for this large and powerful catfish.

Compatibility/Aquarium Behaviour: Highly predatory and usually highly aggressive towards any potential tank mates; best kept alone.

Water Chemistry: Not critical as long as extremes are avoided; a very hardy fish.

Feeding: A greedy feeder that will eat most foods. You can use sinking catfish pellets with meaty foods such as baitfish, mussels, prawn/shrimp and earthworms.

Sexing: No obvious differences between the sexes; females may be fuller bodied.

Breeding: Unlikely in aquaria, due to size and aggression.

BAGRIDAE (Bagrid catfish)
Mystus vittatus
ASIAN-STRIPED CATFISH, PYJAMA CATFISH

20cm
8˝

22-28°C
72-82°F

90cm
36˝

Origin: Asia – Indian subcontinent

Tank Setup: Provide caves using bogwood or rocks for refuge.

Compatibility/Aquarium Behaviour: Not aggressive towards other fish, though small fish may be eaten.

Water Chemistry: Slightly acidic to around neutral pH; soft to medium hard.

Feeding: Eats a range of foods, but prefers meaty, frozen or live foods.

Sexing: No obvious differences between the sexes, but males are usually smaller and more slender and have an elongated genital papilla immediately in front of the anal fin.

Breeding: Few reports of aquarium breeding. The female scatters many thousands of eggs.

CALLICHTHYIDAE (Callichthyid armoured catfish)
Brochis splendens
EMERALD CORY

7cm
3˝

22-28°C
72-82°F

75cm
30˝

Origin: South America – Amazon River basin

Tank Setup: Caves of bogwood or rocks should be provided, along with open areas of soft substrate.

Compatibility/Aquarium Behaviour: A peaceful species that is compatible with any peaceful community fish. Keep in groups.

Water Chemistry: Not too critical, but soft to medium hard with a pH around neutral would be ideal.

Feeding: Sinking pellets and granular foods supplemented with frozen and live food such as bloodworm and brine shrimp.

Sexing: Females are larger and fuller-bodied than males.

Breeding: Spawning is similar to Corydoras. Spawning activity begins with excitable behaviour and the male pursuing the female. She lays eggs on the aquarium glass, other smooth surfaces and plant leaves.

CALLICHTHYIDAE (Callichthyid armoured catfish)
Corydoras aeneus
BRONZE CORY

7,5cm
3″

20-26°C
68-79°F

60cm
24″

Origin: South America

Tank Setup: Planted tank, preferably with a sand substrate.

Compatibility/Aquarium Behaviour: An ideal community fish, peaceful with all other fish.

Water Chemistry: Not critical; neutral pH.

Feeding: Omnivorous; sinking pellets, wafers and granular foods supplemented with frozen and live food.

Sexing: Adult females are larger and more rounded than males.

Breeding: Easy to breed, spawns in typical *Corydoras* fashion (see *Corydoras panda*.)

CALLICHTHYIDAE (Callichthyid armoured catfish)
Corydoras paleatus
PEPPERED CORY

10cm
4″

20-26°C
68-79°F

75cm
30″

Origin: South America – Brazil and Argentina

Tank Setup: Planted tank, preferably with sand or any other suitable smooth substrate.

Compatibility/Aquarium Behaviour: Peaceful and amenable in community tanks.

Water Chemistry: Clear, neutral water

Feeding: Omnivorous; sinking pellets, granular, frozen or live food.

Sexing: Females are larger than males with a more rounded shape.

Breeding: Will spawn easily if the water quality is good, in typical *Corydoras* fashion (see *Corydoras panda*)

CALLICHTHYIDAE (Callichthyid armoured catfish)
Corydoras panda
PANDA CORY

5cm 2"	22-26°C 72-79°F	45cm 18"

Origin: South America – Peru

Tank Setup: Ideally, a planted tank with a few caves formed by bogwood or rocks; soft substrate – fine sand recommended.

Compatibility/Aquarium Behaviour: Peaceful species that can be mixed safely with any other peaceful fish.

Water Chemistry: Fairly soft with slightly acidic to neutral pH is ideal, especially for breeding; tolerate more alkaline water.

Feeding: Small sinking foods such as granular dry foods and sinking catfish pellets supplemented with frozen or live food.

Sexing: Adult females are generally larger and more rounded when viewed from above. No differences apparent in juveniles.

Breeding: Breeds in typical *Corydoras* fashion. Spawning often occurs after a water change, especially with slightly cooler or softer water. Males pursue females, who may begin to clean spawning sites. A pair will then adopt the 'T' position in which the female takes milt from the male to fertilize the eggs she holds in a cup formed by her ventral fins. If you don't remove eggs and young fry after spawning, adults may eat them. Eggs take three to four days to hatch.

CALLICHTHYIDAE (Callichthyid armoured catfish)
Corydoras trilineatus
THREE-LINE CORY

5cm 2"	22-26°C 72-79°F	60cm 24"

Origin: South America – Peru, Brazil, Colombia

Tank Setup: Ideally a planted tank with a sandy substrate or smooth rounded gravel.

Compatibility/Aquarium Behaviour: A peaceful fish; ideal for the community aquarium.

Water Chemistry: Bright, clear water with a pH around neutral.

Feeding: Omnivorous; it prefers live and frozen food, but will take sinking granular and pellet food.

Sexing: Females slightly more robust in build.

Breeding: Spawns in typical Corydoras fashion (*see Corydoras panda*), but quite difficult to spawn.

CALLICHTHYIDAE (Callichthyid armoured catfish)
Dianema urostriatum

12,5cm
5˝

23-28°C
73-82°F

90cm
36˝

FLAG-TAIL PORTHOLE CATFISH

Origin: South America – Brazil

Tank Setup: Provide some caves and plant cover such as some tall and floating plants.

Compatibility/Aquarium Behaviour: Peaceful; best kept in a group.

Water Chemistry: Fairly soft; prefers neutral to slightly acidic water.

Feeding: Will take most dry aquarium foods; supplement with frozen or live foods.

Sexing: Females are fuller-bodied.

Breeding: Reported to be a bubblenest builder and, in some instances, to attach clusters of eggs to surface covers. No available detailed reports of breeding in aquaria.

CALLICHTHYIDAE (Callichthyid armoured catfish)
Megalechis thoracata, formerly Hoplosternum thoracatum

15cm
6˝

18-28°C
64-82°F

90cm
36˝

SPOTTED HOPLO, PORT HOPLO, BUBBLENEST CATFISH

Origin: South America – Amazon and Orinoco river basins, coastal rivers of the Guianas

Tank Setup: A planted tank, include some floating plants.

Compatibility/Aquarium Behaviour: Generally fine for the community tank, although adult fish might eat small tetras.

Water Chemistry: Not critical; soft to medium hard; slightly acidic to slightly alkaline pH.

Feeding: Will take most aquarium foods, including sinking pellets and granular foods. supplement with frozen or live food such as bloodworms.

Sexing: Males have thicker pectoral spines than females. The pectoral spines turn orange-red when in breeding condition.

Breeding: The female lays her eggs in a bubblenest which the male builds and guards. Remove the female after spawning, unless the tank is large enough for her to keep away from the male, which can become quite aggressive.

CLAROTEIDAE
Auchenoglanis occidentalis
GIRAFFE CATFISH

60cm
24″

21-25°C
70-77°F

180cm
72″

Origin: Widespread throughout Africa

Tank Setup: Provide robust décor such as rounded rocks and large pieces of bogwood and a soft sand substrate.

Compatibility/Aquarium Behaviour: Compatible with other suitably sized fish. Mature fish may not tolerate others of their own species.

Water Chemistry: Not critical

Feeding: Omnivorous; will eat most foods. You can use sinking catfish pellets as a staple meal and supplement them with both meaty foods like mussel and vegetable matter.

Sexing: No obvious differences

Breeding: Not reported in aquaria.

DORADIDAE (Thorny catfish)
Agamyxis pectinifrons
SPOTTED-TALKING CATFISH, SPOTTED RAPHAEL

12,5cm
5″

20-26°C
68-79°F

90cm
36″

Origin: South America

Tank Setup: Provide bogwood or small crevices within rockwork for fish to hide. The species prefers dim lighting.

Compatibility/Aquarium Behaviour: Not aggressive towards other fish. However, other fish may eat small fish such as tetras at night when they are resting near the bottom.

Water Chemistry: Not critical; acidic to slightly alkaline water; soft to medium hard.

Feeding: Sinking catfish pellets and frozen or live food that sink quickly.

Sexing: Unknown

Breeding: No details available, may lay its eggs in plants.

DORADIDAE (Thorny catfish)
Megalodoras uranoscopus

– has also been referred to as M. irwini, but this is a junior synonym.

GIANT-TALKING CATFISH, GIANT RAPHAEL, MOTHER OF SNAILS CATFISH

60cm
24″

22-25°C
72-77°F

180cm
72″

Origin: South America – Amazon River basin

Tank Setup: Use robust décor to provide suitable retreats, especially for juveniles.

Compatibility/Aquarium Behaviour: Peaceful towards its own species and other fish. An ideal companion for large fish that use the upper levels of the tank.

Water Chemistry: Not critical as long as you avoid extremes.

Feeding: Omnivorous; feed sinking catfish pellets, tablets and meaty foods such as mussels and earthworms. Also known to feed on snails as one if its common names suggests.

Sexing: Unknown

Breeding: No reports of aquarium spawning

DORADIDAE (Thorny catfish)
Oxydoras niger

– previously known as Pseudodoras niger

BLACK DORID, RIPSAW CATFISH

100cm
39″

21-24°C
70-75°F

240cm
96″

Origin: South America – Amazon region

Tank Setup: A minimum amount of robust décor. You can use large PVC or clay pipes to provide retreats.

Compatibility/Aquarium Behaviour: A true gentle giant, this catfish is not aggressive towards other fish.

Water Chemistry: Not critical; from soft and acidic to medium-hard and alkaline.

Feeding: Omnivorous; feed sinking pellets; tablets; mussels; prawn/ shrimp; earthworms.

Sexing: No obvious differences.

Breeding: Unknown

DORADIDAE (Thorny catfish)
Platydoras costatus
HUMBUG CATFISH, STRIPED RAPHAEL, STRIPED TALKING CATFISH

20cm
8″

23-29°C
73-84°F

90cm
36″

Origin: Widespread in South America

Tank Setup: Provide caves for this fish to rest in during the day as it is mainly nocturnal.

Compatibility/Aquarium Behaviour: Not aggressive towards other fish. May eat small fish such as tetras at night when they are resting near the bottom.

Water Chemistry: Not critical; acidic to slightly alkaline; soft to medium hard.

Feeding: Omnivorous; feed sinking catfish pellets and frozen or live foods. It may be necessary to feed after the aquarium lights go off to ensure it gets its share.

Sexing: Unknown

Breeding: Unknown

LORICARIIDAE (Armoured catfish)
– subfamily: ANCISTRINAE
Ancistrus sp.
BRISTLENOSE CATFISH

12,5cm
5″

21-26°C
70-79°F

75cm
30″

Origin: South America

Tank Setup: Planted tank with enough bogwood refuges for each Bristlenose or similar species.

Compatibility/Aquarium Behaviour: Ideal for the community tank. You may observe some territorial behaviour towards other *Ancistrus*, but this doesn't normally result in any harm. This species is sometimes boisterous towards other bottomfeeders at feeding time.

Water Chemistry: Not critical as this fish is hardy and adaptable. Fairly soft water with neutral to slightly acidic pH is ideal.

Feeding: An excellent algae eater; supplement with algae wafers, sinking pellets and household greens such as blanched lettuce and cucumber. The species will also eat most other foods that midwater dwelling fish have missed.

Sexing: Males have prominent 'bristles' on their heads which give this genus its common name.

Breeding: Will often spawn in the community tank. The male will guard the eggs.

LORICARIIDAE (Armoured catfish)
– subfamily: ANCISTRINAE
Baryancistrus sp.
GOLD NUGGET PLECO, L018/L085, L081, L177

35cm 14″	25-30°C 77-86°F	90cm 36″

Origin: South America

Tank Setup: Provide plenty of bogwood refuge.

Compatibility/Aquarium Behaviour: Territorial towards suckermouth catfish especially Gold Nugget plecos. Compatible with most midwater dwelling fish that do not compete too vigorously for food.

Water Chemistry: Soft to slightly hard; around neutral pH.

Feeding: These fish are omnivorous and not algae eaters as is often assumed with suckermouth catfish. Provide a varied diet including frozen or live foods, dry aquarium food and household vegetables.

Sexing: It is difficult to distinguish the sexes in mature fish, although there are some differences in head shape.

Breeding: Not common in aquaria. A strong current triggers spawning.

LORICARIIDAE (Armoured catfish)
– subfamily: ANCISTRINAE
Hypancistrus zebra
ZEBRA PLECO, L046

7,5cm 3″	25-30°C 77-86°F	75cm 30″

Origin: South America – Brazil, Rio Xingu

Tank Setup: Provide dark-coloured rock or bogwood for refuges. Maintain efficient filtration and good circulation.

Compatibility/Aquarium Behaviour: Peaceful. Do not mix with species that will compete too vigorously for food.

Water Chemistry: Fairly soft to medium hard; pH 6.5-7.6

Feeding: Omnivorous; prefers meaty foods, but does eat green food. This species is not an algae eater.

Sexing: The first ray of the pectoral fin is thicker in the male with odontodes (tiny spines) visible, you can also observe these just below the operculum (gill plate).

Breeding: Maintain the temperature at the upper end of the range. Spawning takes place in small caves. The male will guard his selected cave, which the female then enters. After spawning, the male fertilizes and guards the eggs. It may be wise to hatch the eggs artificially, as the parents may eat the newly hatched fry. Small regular water changes and good oxygenation are necessary. Feed the fry newly hatched brine shrimp.

LORICARIIDAE (Armoured catfish)
– subfamily: ANCISTRINAE
Panaque nigrolineatus
ROYAL PANAQUE, L027, L027A, L027B, L027C, L190

45cm 18″   23-26°C 73-79°F   120cm 48″

Origin: South America

Tank Setup: Provide large pieces of bogwood on which fish can rest.

Compatibility/Aquarium Behaviour: Can be kept with other fish which occupy the upper levels of the tank. Territorial towards its own species.

Water Chemistry: Not critical; fairly soft to slightly hard; acidic to slightly alkaline.

Feeding: Offer a vegetable-based diet in addition to sinking wafers and pellets.

Sexing: Unknown

Breeding: Unknown

LORICARIIDAE (Armoured catfish)
– subfamily: ANCISTRINAE
Pseudacanthicus sp.
SCARLET PLECO, L025

45cm 18″   24-27°C 75-81°F   120cm 48″

Origin: South America

Tank Setup: Provide large pieces of bogwood as the main décor, and preferably subdued lighting.

Compatibility/Aquarium Behaviour: Territorial towards other Loricarids, but can be kept with suitably sized fish that occupy the upper levels of the tank.

Water Chemistry: Slightly acidic to neutral water ideal, but exact pH and hardness values are not criticial.

Feeding: Prefers a carnivorous diet, so provide variety including some meaty foods like mussels, prawns and bloodworms.

Sexing: Males are more slender with more evident spines on the pectoral fins.

Breeding: Unknown

LORICARIIDAE (Armoured catfish)
– subfamily: HYPOPTOPOMATINAE
Otocinclus vittatus
OTO, DWARF SUCKER

4cm 1,5″	21-26°C 70-79°F	45cm 18″

Origin: South America – Brazil

Tank Setup: Provide a mature planted tank with pieces of bog-wood on which fish can rest.

Compatibility/Aquarium Behaviour: Peaceful; keep in a group.

Water Chemistry: Ideally fairly soft, with an acidic to neutral pH (6.0-7.0).

Feeding: A busy algae eater; supplement with other green food and small frozen or live food.

Sexing: Males are smaller and slimmer than females.

Breeding: Rare in aquaria. The female lays eggs on the leaves of plants, and they hatch in about three days. Provide the fry with plenty algae, green and tiny particulate food.

LORICARIIDAE (Armoured catfish)
– subfamily: HYPOSTOMINAE
Hypostomus, Liposarcus or *Pterygoplichthys sp.*
COMMON PLECO

30-50cm 12-20″	20-26°C 68-79°F	120cm 48″

Origin: South America

Tank Setup: Large tank with caves or bogwood for refuge.

Compatibility/Aquarium Behaviour: Generally compatible in a large community tank; may be territorial over a favourite cave.

Water Chemistry: Not critical, tolerates a wide range of pH and hardness values.

Feeding: Generally very good algae eaters; supplement with algae wafers, sinking pellets and green food. They will also con-sume most other foods missed by midwater dwelling fish.

Sexing: No obvious differences between the sexes. Adult males may be smaller than females.

Breeding: Unlikely in the aquarium – in warm climates in out-door ponds the fish dig tunnels in which to spawn.

LORICARIIDAE (Armoured catfish)
– subfamily: LORICARIINAE
Farlowella acus
TWIG CATFISH

20cm
8″

20-25°C
68-77°F

90cm
36″

Origin: South America

Tank Setup: Provide plenty of bogwood or twigs and branches. Plants are optional. Subdued lighting preferred.

Compatibility/Aquarium Behaviour: A relatively timid species which should be kept with non-aggressive fish such as *Corydoras* and tetras.

Water Chemistry: Ideally fairly soft, with an acidic to slightly alkaline pH.

Feeding: Supply algae and other green foods along with frozen or live food and sinking tablets and wafers.

Sexing: Males grow pronounced bristles.

Breeding: The male cleans a surface and then guards the eggs laid there by the female. Fry can be difficult to feed, but benefit from being reared in a mature planted aquarium where there is likely to be a supply of natural microscopic food.

Adding fish to your aquarium

When adding fish to the tank, switch off the aquarium lighting and allow the bag with the new fish to float in the tank for at least 15 minutes; this will equalize the water temperature in the bag. You could instead also open the top of the bag and allow some aquarium water to mix with the water in the bag. Leave the bag for 5-10 minutes and then repeat this a couple more times. The bag can then be tilted gently to allow the fish to swim out.

Where there is a large difference in water chemistry between that of the supplier and that of your own tank release the fish from their bags into a clean bucket with the bag water. Using a length of standard airline, siphon water from the main tank into the bucket, but slow it down first to a drip using a small plastic airline clamp. Allow the bucket to fill over several hours and then either net or rebag the fish to add them to the tank.

MALAPTERURIDAE (Electric catfish)
Malapterurus electricus
ELECTRIC CATFISH

120cm
48″

23-29°C
73-84°F

150cm
60″

Size: Reported to be up to 120cm (48in), but usually considerably smaller in aquaria less than 60cm (24in).

Origin: Central Africa including Lake Tanganyika

Tank Setup: Provide a suitable retreat in the way of a large PVC or clay pipe. Heaters should have a guard, or preferably be external.

Compatibility/Aquarium Behaviour: Should be kept alone as a single specimen where it makes for an interesting 'pet' fish.

Water Chemistry: Not critical; neutral to alkaline pH; medium to hard water.

Feeding: Takes most meaty foods such as mussels, baitfish, earthworms and prawn/shrimp. Beware of overfeeding, especially in adult fish.

Sexing: Males are more slender.

Breeding: It is reported that the fish spawn in pits, but there are no accounts of breeding in aquaria.

MOCHOKIDAE (Upside-down catfish)
Synodontis decorus
CLOWN SYNO

30cm
12″

22-28°C
72-82°F

120°cm
48″

Origin: Africa – Congo basin

Tank Setup: Provide bogwood or rocks to form caves. A soft sand substrate is preferable.

Compatibility/Aquarium Behaviour: Generally suitable for a large community tank, where it holds its own with most large fish. Likely to be territorial with other *Synodontis* catfish.

Water Chemistry: Not critical; a wide range of pH and hardness values are suitable, as long as you avoid extremes.

Feeding: Eats crustacea, algae and insect larvae in the wild, but like many Synodontis species it will scavenge for aquarium food. A good staple diet comprises sinking catfish pellets.

Sexing: No obvious external differences between the sexes, without resorting to examination of the genital papillae. Males are more slender in shape.

Breeding: Unknown in the aquarium.

MOCHOKIDAE (Upside-down catfish)
Synodontis multipunctatus
CUCKOO CATFISH

15cm
6″

22-29°C
72-79°F

90cm
36″

Origin: Eastern Africa – Lake Tanganyika

Tank Setup: Lots of rocky décor to provide plenty of caves, particularly if kept with Rift lake cichlids.

Compatibility/Aquarium Behaviour: Usually kept with cichlids of Malawi and Tanganyika. Slightly territorial towards its own species, but much less so than many *Synodontis* species.

Water Chemistry: Hard and alkaline, pH 7.5-8.5

Feeding: Insectivorous; prefers live or frozen food, but will accept flakes and tablets. Snail eater.

Sexing: Males tend to be smaller with a higher dorsal fin and may have longer pectoral spines. Like other *Synodontis*, it may also be possible to see a short papillae close to the males vent.

Breeding: The common name of 'Cuckoo' derives from the habit of this catfish, that of swimming between spawning cichlids, eating their eggs and depositing their own. The mouthbrooding female cichlid then picks up the eggs and raises the resulting fry alongside her own fry. This often results in the faster-growing catfish fry eating the cichlid fry.

MOCHOKIDAE (Upside-down catfish)
Synodontis nigriventris
TRUE UPSIDE-DOWN CATFISH

10cm
4″

22-27°C
72-84°F

75cm
30″

Origin: Africa – Congo basin

Tank Setup: Planted tank with bogwood or branches to allow fish to rest upside-down.

Compatibility/Aquarium Behaviour: A peaceful catfish well suited to the community tank.

Water Chemistry: Not critical; slightly acidic to slightly alkaline and fairly soft water would be ideal.

Feeding: Will eat most aquarium foods. Provide granular, flake and pellet food and supplement with frozen and live food like bloodworms and brine shrimp (*Artemia*).

Sexing: The female has a larger and more rounded profile than the male.

Breeding: No detailed reports, although there have been incidental spawnings in aquaria.

MOCHOKIDAE (Upside-down catfish)
Synodontis flavitaeniatus
PYJAMA SYNO, ORANGE-STRIPED SYNO, GOLD-STRIPED SYNO

20cm
8″

24-28°C
75-82°F

90cm
36″

Origin: Africa – central Congo area

Tank Setup: Provide a sandy substrate and refuge in the way of bogwood or rock caves.

Compatibility/Aquarium Behaviour: A relatively peaceful Synodontis that you can combine with other similarly sized fish.

Water Chemistry: Not critical; soft to medium hard water with a neutral to alkaline pH.

Feeding: Omnivorous; will eat sinking granular and pellet food; supplement with frozen or live food.

Sexing: No obvious differences

Breeding: Has been bred in captivity; no details available.

PIMELODIDAE
(Long-whiskered catfish)
Brachyplatystoma juruense
ZEBRA CATFISH, POOR MAN'S TIGRINUS, BANDED SHOVELNOSE

60cm
24″

22-27°C
72-84°F

150cm
60″

Origin: South America – Amazon and Orinoco river basins

Tank Setup: Provide a moderate current and smooth rocks and large pieces of bogwood for décor.

Compatibility/Aquarium Behaviour: Highly predatory; keep only with fish that are too large to fit in its mouth.

Water Chemistry: A pH value around neutral; soft to medium-hard water is suitable.

Feeding: Predatory; feed meaty foods such as mussels, prawns, whitebait and earthworms.

Sexing: Unknown

Breeding: Unknown

PIMELODIDAE
(Long-whiskered catfish)
Leiarius pictus
SAILFIN MARBLED PIM

| 60cm 24″ | 22-26°C 72-79°F | 240cm 96″ |

Origin: South America

Tank Setup: Minimal décor to leave plenty of swimming space.

Compatibility/Aquarium Behaviour: Very territorial towards other Pimelodidae catfish. The larger Doradid catfish are probably the best choice for companions from the catfish family. You could add large peaceful shoaling fish in a large aquarium.

Water Chemistry: Not critical; fairly soft water with a slightly acidic to neutral pH is ideal.

Feeding: Eats almost any food including sinking catfish pellets and floating sticks, which it will take from the surface. Offer meaty foods such as mussels, baitfish, prawn/shrimp and earthworms.

Sexing: No obvious differences between the sexes; females may be bulkier.

Breeding: Not reported in aquaria, no doubt due to the enormous tank that would be required to house and spawn a pair.

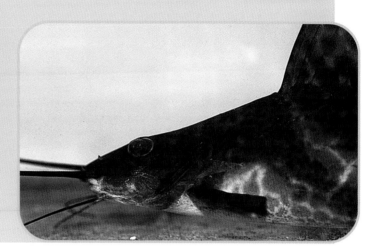

Protection of fry

Some fish, most notably cichlids, but also other groups, do not leave the survival of their eggs and fry to chance, but protect them. There are many different variations of this. Sometimes one parent is the guardian, sometimes both are. Sometimes the female lays eggs in pits, caves, or 'nests' comprising bubbles and surface vegetation. Some fish, again notably many cichlids, practise 'mouthbrooding' where one (or occasionally both) of the parents incubate the eggs and/or protect the fry inside their mouths. While there are often only a small number of fry, this protection gives them a very good start in life.

PIMELODIDAE
(Long-whiskered catfish)
Phractocephalus hemioliopterus
RED-TAILED CATFISH

120cm
48″

21-27°C
71-80°F

240cm
96″

Origin: South America – Amazon

Tank Setup: Requires a huge tank; 240 x 90 x 90cm (8 x 3 x 3 feet) is considered a minimum for an adult. Décor should be minimal, and comprise robust items that it cannot swallow or bash against the tank glass. Preferably keep heaters and filtration outside of the main aquarium (a sump filter is ideal).

Compatibility/Aquarium Behaviour: Highly predatory, this huge catfish will try to swallow any fish that appears small enough – it may even swallow inanimate objects such as heaters! Although territorial with other Pimelodid catfish, you can keep it with other very large tank mates, though in practice, only public aquaria normally have tanks large enough for this.

Water Chemistry: Not critical; fairly soft to medium-hard; pH 6.8-7.6

Feeding: Carnivorous; feed catfish pellets, mussels, prawn/shrimp, whitebait; move on to larger fish as the catfish grows.

Sexing: No clear differences between the sexes, but males may have a deeper red tail and possess a more slender shape.

Breeding: Unknown, and impractical in home aquaria.

PIMELODIDAE
(Long-whiskered catfish)
Pimelodus pictus
SPOTTED PIM, PICTUS CAT, ANGEL PIM.

12,5cm
5″

22-25°C
72-77°F

90cm
36″

Origin: South America – Peru and Colombia

Tank Setup: Plenty of open swimming space with bogwood or rocks to form caves for refuge.

Compatibility/Aquarium Behaviour: A predator that will eat small aquarium fish such as slim-bodied tetras. Not aggressive towards larger fish. They will show some territoriality towards their own kind; best kept in groups.

Water Chemistry: Fairly soft and slightly acidic; pH 6.0-6.8 is ideal, but tolerates a wide range of hardness and pH values.

Feeding: Carnivorous/insectivorous; will take various flakes, pellets and frozen or live foods in the aquarium.

Sexing: No differences known.

Breeding: Not reported in aquaria.

SILURIDAE (Sheatfish)
Kryptopterus minor
ASIAN GLASS CATFISH, GHOST CATFISH

8cm
3″

22-27°C
72-81°F

75cm
30″

Origin: India and Southeast Asia

Tank Setup: A planted tank with open swimming space; floating plants provide shade. Water flow should be gentle.

Compatibility/Aquarium Behaviour: A peaceful shoaling catfish that should always be in a group.

Water Chemistry: Fairly soft; a slightly acidic pH is ideal.

Feeding: Prefers live or frozen foods; may take dry aquarium food once settled.

Sexing: Unknown

Breeding: There are no detailed reports of aquarium breeding available.

Characins

Characins originate mainly from South America, but around 200 species are also found in Africa. The most familiar characins are the species known as 'Tetras'. Most of these are small and colourful and make ideal aquarium fish. At the other end of the scale are fish such as the Pacu, which grow very large and are only really suitable for public aquaria. Some characins are quite specialized, such as the remarkable Hatchetfish, which are capable of leaping from the water to escape predators.

The Characins also include the infamous Piranhas, a group of fish familiar even to most non-fishkeepers. These fish have a somewhat exaggerated reputation, and are often purchased for the wrong reasons, but deserve respect nonetheless. Other predatory characins include the Pike Characins and Wolf Fish (Erythrinidae).

A feature shared by most Characins (except Erythrinidae) is the presence of an adipose fin between the dorsal and caudal (tail) fins. This feature is not found on Cyprinid fish such as barbs, and serves as an extra means of identification.

ALESTIIDAE (African tetras)
Arnoldichthys spilopterus
RED-EYED CHARACIN

8cm
3″

24-28°C
75-82°F

90cm
36″

Origin: Western Africa

Tank Setup: Plants and wood towards the back and sides of the tank, with plenty of open swimming space.

Compatibility/Aquarium Behaviour: An active, but peaceful tetra that is best kept with other fast-moving shoaling fish and bottomfeeders such as small Synodontis catfish and loaches.

Water Chemistry: pH around neutral, soft to slightly hard.

Feeding: Flakes and granular foods; supplement with frozen and live food.

Sexing: The anal fin of the male is convex with red, yellow and black stripes. The anal fin of the female is straighter with a black tip.

Breeding: Egg-scatterer, which may lay more than 1000 eggs.

ALESTIIDAE (African tetras)
Phenacogrammus interruptus
CONGO TETRA

8cm
3″

23-27°C
73-81°F

90cm
36″

Origin: Central Africa – Congo

Tank Setup: A well-planted tank with plenty of swimming space. A dark substrate and/or background will show off their colours to best effect.

Compatibility/Aquarium Behaviour: A peaceful shoaling fish; do not keep with very boisterous fish that compete strongly for food. May eat much smaller tetras such as Neons.

Water Chemistry: Prefers fairly soft and slightly acidic water, but not essential.

Feeding: Flakes and granular food; supplement with frozen and live food.

Sexing: The male is larger and more colourful than the female, with an extended dorsal and tail fin.

Breeding: Likely to spawn in the morning, especially if triggered by sunlight. Use soft and acidic water at the upper end of the temperature range. Usually spawns in shoals, scattering a few hundred eggs in the lower regions of the tank. Fry hatch after about six days.

ANOSTOMIDAE (Headstanders)
Abramites hypselonotus
MARBLED HEADSTANDER, HIGH-BACKED HEADSTANDER

12,5cm
5˝

23-26°C
73-79°F

90cm
36˝

Origin: Amazon and Orinoco river basins

Tank Setup: Use bogwood and stones for décor, along with artificial plants if desired; live plants are likely to be eaten quickly.

Compatibility/Aquarium Behaviour: Can combine with similar-sized fish, but adults are intolerant of their own kind.

Water Chemistry: Fairly soft, slightly acidic to neutral water ideal, but not essential.

Feeding: Herbivorous; vegetable and spirulina-based flakes, household greens; also feed frozen or live foods occasionally to vary the diet.

Sexing: Unknown

Breeding: No reports of aquarium breeding.

ANOSTOMIDAE (Headstanders)
Anostomus anostomus
STRIPED ANOSTOMUS

18cm
7˝

22-28°C
72-82°F

90cm
36˝

Origin: South America – Amazon and Orinoco river basins

Tank Setup: Use rocks and wood for décor; artificial or robust live plants provide vertically orientated retreats. Provide good circulation and bright lighting.

Compatibility/Aquarium Behaviour: Territorial towards their own kind, so keep a single specimen or a large group in a big tank. Not usually aggressive towards other fish.

Water Chemistry: Fairly soft to medium hard, with an acidic to slightly alkaline pH.

Feeding: Omnivorous; feed a variety of dry and frozen or live foods. Include vegetables in the diet.

Sexing: Differences in sexes unknown; females may be deeper bodied.

Breeding: Rarely achieved in aquaria; no details available.

CHARACIDAE (Characins)
Chalceus macrolepidotus
PINK-TAILED CHALCEUS

| 25cm 10″ | 23-27°C 73-82°F | 150cm 60″ |

Origin: South America – Guyana, Suriname and French Guiana

Tank Setup: Requires a large tank with plenty of open swimming space, but provide shelter with large pieces of wood and tall plants.

Compatibility/Aquarium Behaviour: Predatory; keep with large fish.

Water Chemistry: Not critical; fairly soft to medium-hard water with an approximate neutral pH value (6.5-7.5).

Feeding: Carnivorous; feed live and dead meaty foods; young fish will take flakes and pellets.

Sexing: Differences between the sexes unknown.

Breeding: No reports of aquarium breeding.

CHARACIDAE (Characins)
Exodon paradoxus
BUCKTOOTH TETRA

| 15cm 6″ | 23-28°C 72-82°F | 90cm 36″ |

Size: Up to 15cm (6in), but usually 10cm (4in).

Origin: South America – Amazon and Tocantins river basins

Tank Setup: Species tank with plenty of plants and wood.

Compatibility/Aquarium Behaviour: Not suitable for general community tanks! May remove scales and bite fins of other fish. It is best to keep it in a species tank, although armoured catfish (Loricarids) and cichlids may prove suitable tank mates. Aggressive with its own kind; keep in large numbers (suggest more than 10) to dissipate aggression.

Water Chemistry: pH around neutral; soft to medium hard.

Feeding: Carnivorous; feed frozen and live meaty foods.

Sexing: Females are larger and broader than males.

Breeding: Not often accomplished in aquaria. The female scatters the eggs among the plants. You should remove the adult fish after spawning.

CHARACIDAE (Charagins)
Gymnocorymbus ternetzi
BLACK WIDOW TETRA

5cm
2″

21-27°C
70-82°F

75cm
30″

Origin: South America – Brazil and Paraguay

Tank Setup: A planted tank, with open swimming space.

Compatibility/Aquarium Behaviour: Usually a peaceful community fish, although it has been known to nip the fins of long-finned fish. Conversely, long-finned varieties of this species may attract the attention of fin nippers.

Water Chemistry: Tolerates a wide range, but prefers soft and slightly acidic (pH 6.0-7.0) water.

Feeding: Omnivorous; flakes, frozen and live food.

Sexing: Females are slightly larger than the males and have rounder bodies. Males may show white spots on their tail fins.

Breeding: Females scatter eggs among fine-leaved plants, which hatch in about a day. Typical of egg-scatterers, parents will eat the eggs if given the opportunity.

CHARACIDAE (CHARACINS)
Hemigrammus bleheri
RUMMY-NOSE TETRA, RED-NOSE TETRA, FIREHEAD TETRA

5cm
2″

23-26°C
73-79°F

75cm
30″

Origin: South America – Brazil and Colombia

Tank Setup: A planted tank with some open swimming space for this active shoaler.

Compatibility/Aquarium Behaviour: A peaceful community fish that you can mix safely with other peaceful fish. Do not mix slim tetras such as the Rummy Nose with potentially predatory species.

Water Chemistry: Fairly soft with slightly acidic to neutral pH would be ideal, though captive bred fish in particular can be maintained in moderately hard and alkaline water without problems.

Feeding: Eats most aquarium foods, supplement dry food with small frozen or live food.

Sexing: The colour of the male and female is identical, but the female is larger.

Breeding: Very difficult. Requires soft and acidic water.

CHARACIDAE (Characins)
Hyphessobrycon anisitsi
— *often known as Hemigrammus caudovittatus – a junior synonym.*

BUENOS AIRES TETRA

7,5cm
3˝

18-28°C
64-82°F

90cm
36˝

Origin: South America – Argentina, Brazil and Paraguay

Tank Setup: Provide this lively shoaling fish with plenty of open swimming space. You can add robust plants, but the species is likely to eat soft-leaved varieties.

Compatibility/Aquarium Behaviour: A very active, but normally peaceful species; may show some aggression towards smaller, more timid tetras; long-finned fish may be nipped.

Water Chemistry: Not critical, a very hardy species.

Feeding: Omnivorous; feed flakes and granular foods along with some live or frozen foods; also include vegetables.

Sexing: Males are slimmer than females, and often show more vivid colours.

Breeding: A relatively easy tetra to breed. Temperature for spawning should be in the middle to upper end of the range quoted above. Spawning takes place over plants and the eggs hatch in about one day.

CHARACIDAE (Characins)
Hemigrammus erythrozonus
GLOWLIGHT TETRA

4cm
1,5˝

22-26°C
72-79°F

60cm
24˝

Origin: South America – Guyana

Tank Setup: A well-planted tank, preferably with a dark substrate and/or background, which will display the colour of the species to its best advantage.

Compatibility/Aquarium Behaviour: A peaceful species, well suited to the community tank.

Water Chemistry: Acidic to slightly alkaline (pH 6.0-7.5); soft to slightly hard.

Feeding: Omnivorous; feed flakes and small live or frozen food.

Sexing: Males are noticeably slimmer than the females.

Breeding: Requires soft, acidic water. Spawns over fine-leaved plants.

CHARACIDAE (Characins)
Hyphessobrycon erythrostigma
BLEEDING HEART TETRA

| 7,5cm | 23-28°C | 75cm |
| 3″ | 73-82°F | 30″ |

Origin: South America – upper Amazon basin

Tank Setup: A planted aquarium with some wood to break up the décor.

Compatibility/Aquarium Behaviour: A peaceful community fish

Water Chemistry: Prefers soft and acidic water.

Feeding: Omnivorous; small live and frozen foods; flakes

Sexing: Males are slimmer than females and have a significantly extended dorsal fin and a more pointed anal fin.

Breeding: An egg-scatterer, which has proven very difficult to breed in aquaria.

CHARACIDAE (Characins)
Hyphessobrycon flammeus
FLAME TETRA

| 4,5cm | 23-27°C | 60cm |
| 1,5″ | 73-81°F | 24″ |

Origin: South America – Brazil

Tank Setup: A well-planted tank. Subdued lighting and a dark background will show off this species' red colour to its best advantage.

Compatibility/Aquarium Behaviour: Usually a peaceful community fish, with only very occasional reports of antisocial behaviour towards more timid species.

Water Chemistry: Fairly soft to slightly hard with an acidic to neutral pH.

Feeding: Flakes, frozen and live food.

Sexing: The female has less intense colour on her anal fin than the male does, and has black tips on her pectoral fins. The male is slimmer than the female.

Breeding: Spawns in typical tetra fashion by scattering eggs over plants.

CHARACIDAE (Characins)
Hyphessobrycon herbertaxelrodi
BLACK NEON TETRA

5cm
2″

23-27°C
73-81°F

60cm
24″

Origin: South America – Mato Grosso area of Brazil

Tank Setup: Planted tank with open shoaling space. Subdued lighting or shade from floating plants will accentuate the colours of the fish.

Compatibility/Aquarium Behaviour: A peaceful fish for a community tank with other similarly peaceful fish. Keep in a shoal.

Water Chemistry: Not critical, but prefers soft and slightly acidic water, especially for breeding.

Feeding: Omnivorous; feed flakes and small granular food; supplement with frozen and live food.

Sexing: The female has a deeper and more rounded body than the male.

Breeding: An egg-scatterer which spawns fairly readily in soft and acidic water. Eggs take just over a day to hatch.

CHARACIDAE (Characins)
Hyphessobrycon sweglesi
– previously known as Megalamphodus sweglesi
RED PHANTOM TETRA

5cm
2″

20-25°C
68-77°F

60cm
24″

Origin: South America – Orinoco River basin

Tank Setup: Planted tank.

Compatibility/Aquarium Behaviour: A peaceful species that is ideal for the community aquarium; keep in a shoal.

Water Chemistry: Prefers soft and acidic water, but tolerates harder and more alkaline water well.

Feeding: Flakes and small frozen or live food.

Sexing: Males have a longer red-coloured dorsal fin than females; in females the dorsal is red, black and white.

Breeding: Requires soft and acidic water with subdued lighting and a cooler temperature than is often used for spawning tetras.

CHARACIDAE (Characins)
Moenkhausia sanctaefilomenae
RED-EYE TETRA

7,5cm
3″

22-26°C
72-79°F

75cm
30″

Origin: South America – Bolivia, Brazil, Paraguay and eastern Peru

Tank Setup: Planted tank, with plenty of open swimming space.

Compatibility/Aquarium Behaviour: A very lively species, well suited to a large community tank. Avoid small timid fish or those with long fins.

Water Chemistry: Not critical for this hardy tetra; soft to medium hard, pH 6.0-7.8.

Feeding: Omnivorous; eagerly accepts most aquarium foods; include vegetables.

Sexing: Males appear slimmer in mature groups.

Breeding: An egg-scatterer that will spawn in pairs or groups among fine plants or the roots of floating plants. Eggs hatch in one to two days.

CHARACIDAE (Characins)
Paracheirodon axelrodi
CARDINAL TETRA

5cm
2″

22-26°C
72-79°F

60cm
24″

Origin: South America – Brazil, Columbia and Venezuela

Tank Setup: A well-planted tank; add some dark wood to the décor to show this fish off to its full potential.

Compatibility/Aquarium Behaviour: Peaceful community fish

Water Chemistry: Prefers very soft and acidic water, but captive-bred stock tolerates slightly harder and alkaline water well.

Feeding: Omnivorous; flakes; granular food – supplement with small live and frozen food.

Sexing: Males are slimmer than females.

Breeding: Requires very soft (3° GH), acidic water. Remove the parents after spawning, which usually occurs in the evening. The female lays approximately 500 eggs, which will hatch in about 24 hours.

CHARACIDAE (Characins)
Paracheirodon innesi
NEON TETRA

4,5cm	22-26°C	60cm
1,5″	72-79°F	24″

Origin: South America – Peru

Tank Setup: A planted tank with a dark substrate and/or background, will best accentuate the colours of the fish.

Compatibility/Aquarium Behaviour: A peaceful community fish whose larger tank mates may eat it. It is best to keep it with other small tetras, Corydoras catfish and small Loricarids (suckermouth catfish).

Water Chemistry: Approximately neutral; soft to medium hard.

Feeding: Omnivorous – flakes, micropellets and small frozen or live food.

Sexing: Males are slimmer than the females, which have deeper bodies.

Breeding: Very soft and acidic water is recommended for breeding purposes, although there are reports of this species being bred in harder water. You can use Java Moss, other fine-leaved plants, or a synthetic equivalent as a spawning substrate.

You should remove the parents after spawning. The eggs hatch in approximately 24 hours. You can initially feed the tiny fry infusoria, and then brine shrimp nauplii.

CHARACIDAE (Characins)
– subfamily: SERRASALMINAE
Metynnis hypsauchen
SILVER DOLLAR

15cm	24-28°C	90cm
6″	75-82°F	36″

Origin: South America – Amazon and Paraguay river basins

Tank Setup: Large tank with wood for décor, and plenty of open swimming space. Plants should be artificial or very robust types such as Java Fern, as most plants will be eaten.

Compatibility/Aquarium Behaviour: Generally peaceful, best kept with other larger community fish. Also suitable as dither fish for medium-large cichlids.

Water Chemistry: Not too critical, but prefers soft, slightly acidic water.

Feeding: Accepts most foods, but the diet should consist mainly of vegetable matter.

Sexing: The anal fin of the male is longer than that of the female, and is usually a brighter red with black edging.

Breeding: May spawn in pairs or shoals. Soft tannin-stained water is recommended and, initially, subdued lighting (an increase in the lighting levels may trigger spawning). Females lay eggs among clumps of plants.

CHARACIDAE (Characins)
– subfamily: SERRASALMINAE
Myleus schomburgkii
BLACK BARRED DOLLAR

15cm
6˝

23-27°C
73-81°F

120cm
48˝

Origin: South America – Amazon and Orinoco river basins

Tank Setup: A large tank with wood for décor, and plastic or robust live plants. This species will eat most soft-leaved plants.

Compatibility/Aquarium Behaviour: Generally peaceful and suitable for the large community aquarium.

Water Chemistry: Prefers soft acidic water, but this is not essential.

Feeding: Herbivorous – feed vegetable-based flakes or pellets and fruit and vegetables.

Sexing: The anal fin of the male is bi-lobed and elongated; the anal fin of the female is shorter and wider than that of the male. The dorsal fin of the male is also said to be longer and more pointed.

Breeding: No reports of aquarium breeding.

CHARACIDAE (Characins)
– subfamily: SERRASALMINAE
Piaractus brachypomus
RED PACU, PIRAPITINGA

80cm
32˝

22-26°C
72-79°F

240cm
96˝

Origin: South America – Amazon and Orinoco river basins

Tank Setup: A very large tank of more than 200 gallons.

Compatibility/Aquarium Behaviour: Usually fairly peaceful for its size, can keep it with other 'tankbuster' fish in a large aquarium – preferably a public aquarium.

Water Chemistry: Acidic to neutral pH (5.5-7.0), but not critical as this species will thrive in a wide variety of conditions.

Feeding: Omnivorous; will eat most large foods.

Sexing: Unknown

Breeding: Unlikely in aquaria

CHARACIDAE (Characins)
– subfamily: SERRASALMINAE
Pygocentrus nattereri
RED-BELLIED PIRANHA

30cm 12″	24-27°C 75-81°F	120cm 48″

Origin: South America including large areas of the Amazon and its major tributaries

Tank Setup: A large tank with bogwood, and a few robust or plastic plants for décor. Subdued lighting. A shoal of adults will require a tank of 100-gallons plus. Heavy-duty filtration is essential.

Compatibility/Aquarium Behaviour: A highly predatory carnivore; keep in a shoal in a species tank.

Water Chemistry: Fairly soft, slightly acidic water (pH 6.0-6.9) is preferable, but not essential.

Feeding: Live or dead meaty foods. (It is not necessary to use live feeder fish, as you can wean this species onto suitable alternatives like mussels, prawns, baitfish and earthworms.)

Sexing: There are no clear differences between the sexes, but breeding females have a more robust shape.

Breeding: The female lays eggs among plants or in a pit in the substrate and defends them with the male. Hatching takes about two to three days.

CHARACIDAE (Characins)
– subfamily: SERRASALMINAE
Serrasalmus rhombeus – incorrectly known as S. niger.
BLACK PIRANHA

40cm 16″	24-27°C 75-81°F	120cm 48″

Origin: South America – Amazon basin and Guyana

Tank Setup: A large tank with bogwood, and possibly a few robust or plastic plants for décor. An adult will require a tank of 100 gallons or more. Heavy-duty filtration is essential. The species prefers dim lighting.

Compatibility/Aquarium Behaviour: A highly predatory and aggressive carnivore; keep alone.

Water Chemistry: Soft, acidic water (pH 5.8-6.8), but not essential.

Feeding: Meaty foods; normally takes thawed fish such as whitebait, along with earthworms and other meaty foods such as mussels. Initially, many young specimens refuse to eat during daylight hours, especially in more brightly illuminated tanks.

Sexing: The anal fin of the male is extended at the front, on females it is straight.

Breeding: The females lays eggs among plants or in a pit in the substrate and defends them with the male. Hatching takes around two to three days.

CITHARINIDAE
Distichodus sexfasciatus
SIX-BARRED DISTICHODUS

75cm
30˝

22-26°C
72-79°F

150cm
60˝

Size: 75cm (30in), but usually much smaller in aquaria about 38cm (15in).

Origin: Africa, Congo and Lake Tanganyika

Tank Setup: You can use large plastic plants and wood for décor; the species will eat live plants. Leave plenty of open swimming space.

Compatibility/Aquarium Behaviour: Aggressive towards their own kind, so it is best to keep them alone unless you can provide a huge aquarium for a large group. Avoid adding nervous mid-water fish like Silver Sharks and Tinfoil Barbs, as the *Distichodus sexfasciatus* may harass them. Large cichlids and catfish are good tank mates for larger specimens.

Water Chemistry: Not critical; fairly soft to very hard, pH 6.0-8.5.

Feeding: Herbivorous; provide plenty of vegetable matter in the form of vegetable-based flakes and pellets, and household vegetables and greens.

Sexing: No obvious differences between the sexes, but females are more heavy bodied.

Breeding: Unknown in aquaria.

CTENOLUCIIDAE (Pike characids)
Boulengerella maculata
SPOTTED PIKE-CHARACIN

35cm
14˝

23-27°C
73-81°F

120cm
48˝

Origin: South America – Amazon, Tocantins and Orinoco rivers

Tank Setup: You can use tall plants; leave plenty of open swimming space at the surface. Floating plants will help to discourage this fish from jumping, but do not reduce the swimming space on the surface too much.

Compatibility/Aquarium Behaviour: Predatory; will eat small fish. Not aggressive towards other larger fish. Avoid adding aggressive fish that use the upper levels of the tank, as this species is startled easily and may injure itself.

Water Chemistry: Acidic to slightly alkaline (pH 6.0-7.2); soft to slightly hard water.

Feeding: Carnivorous; feed frozen or live meaty foods. It is difficult to wean this predator onto aquarium food and you may need to be patient. Allowing the current to carry food items past them from the filter output is a good way to encourage them to feed on non-live food.

Sexing: Differences between the sexes are unknown; females may be larger and deeper bodied.

Breeding: Not known in aquaria.

ERYTHRINIDAE (Trahiras)
Erythrinus erythrinus
RED WOLF FISH

20cm 8″	22-26°C 72-79°F	90cm 36″

Origin: South America

Tank Setup: Provide bogwood or rocks to form caves – PVC or clay pipes are also favoured as retreats. You can include plants. Make sure the tank has a tight-fitting cover, as these fish can escape the aquarium.

Compatibility/Aquarium Behaviour: Highly predatory and can be aggressive, especially to fish that are similar in appearance.

Water Chemistry: Not critical.

Feeding: Carnivorous; feed baitfish, mussels, prawn/shrimp and earthworms. Young fish will take frozen or live bloodworms. Some individuals will take pellets.

Sexing: Unknown

Breeding: Not known in aquaria.

ERYTHRINIDAE (Trahiras)
Hoplias malabaricus
WOLF FISH, TIGER FISH, MUD CHARACIN, TRAHIRA

50cm 20″	21-25°C 70-77°F	120cm 48″

Origin: Central and South America

Tank Setup: Use a tank with a fairly large base area – the height is not as important. This species is not overly active, so very large tanks are unnecessary. You can use a few robust or artificial plants, and pieces of bogwood or rounded stones for décor.

Compatibility/Aquarium Behaviour: Highly predatory, keep alone or with larger fish. May attack and eat fish almost its own size. Can be very aggressive and has a powerful bite. Care should be taken when cleaning the aquarium, as the fish may retaliate if cornered or frightened.

Water Chemistry: Not critical; this fish is hardy and adaptable.

Feeding: Carnivorous; live and dead meaty food such as bait-fish, mussels and earthworms. Do not feed adults everyday, especially if you maintain the aquarium water at the lower end of the temperature range.

Sexing: Males are slimmer and have less curved ventral profiles than females.

Breeding: Has been bred in captivity on rare occasions; difficult due to aggression.

CICHLIDAE (Cichlids)
Labidochromis caeruleus
YELLOW LAB, ELECTRIC YELLOW, CANARY CICHLID

10cm
4″

22-28°C
73-82°F

90cm
36″

Origin: Africa – Lake Malawi

Tank Setup: Typical rocky Malawi tank.

Compatibility/Aquarium Behaviour: Combine with other mbuna species; not overly aggressive.

Water Chemistry: Hard and alkaline; pH 7.6-8.6; GH 7° plus; KH 10-12°

Feeding: Small crustaceans and insect larvae; will accept most aquarium food.

Sexing: No obvious colour differences between males and females are apparent, but dominant males usually show more black on their fins, particularly their ventral fins, and may also exhibit a brown patch in the area between their eyes and mouths.

Breeding: Mouthbrooder; there is no defined territory for spawning.

CICHLIDAE (Cichlids)
Melanochromis auratus
MALAWI GOLDEN CICHLID

12,5cm
5″

23-28°C
73-82°F

120cm
48″

Origin: Africa – Lake Malawi, southern areas of the lake.

Tank Setup: A large tank with many rock caves to allow females and weaker fish to find a safe haven.

Compatibility/Aquarium Behaviour: A very aggressive mbuna; combine them with other larger mbuna species. Do not attempt to keep more than one male per tank (or similar males of other *Melanochromis* species).

Water Chemistry: Hard and alkaline; pH 7.6-8.6; GH 7° plus; KH 10-12°

Feeding: Omnivorous; feeds on algae and the organisms within it. Will accept most aquarium foods; include a lot of vegetables in the diet.

Sexing: Juveniles and females show their distinctive yellow-and-black horizontal stripes; older males are much darker in colour.

Breeding: Mouthbrooder. Keep at least three females to prevent an aggressive male persistently harassing a single female.

CICHLIDAE (Cichlids)

Metriaclima estherae – also known as *Maylandia estherae*.

RED ZEBRA

10–12.5cm
4–5˝

23-28°C
73-82°F

45cm
18˝

Origin: Africa – Lake Malawi, eastern coast

Tank Setup: A large tank with many rock caves

Compatibility/Aquarium Behaviour: Combine with other mbuna species.

Water Chemistry: Hard and alkaline; pH 7.6-8.6; GH 7° plus; KH 10-12°

Feeding: Omnivorous; normally feeds on *aufwuchs* and plankton; include vegetables in the diet.

Sexing: Wild males are blue to white in colour, while the females are beige to brown or orange; an OB morph also occurs.

Breeding: Mouthbrooder; males will defend a spawning site around a cave.

CICHLIDAE (Cichlids)

Pseudotropheus saulosi

NO COMMON NAME IN WIDESPREAD USE

7,5cm
3˝

23-28°C
73-82°F

90cm
36˝

Origin: Africa – Lake Malawi, endemic to the Taiwan Reef area

Tank Setup: Typical mbuna tank with many rock caves.

Compatibility/Aquarium Behaviour: Not overly aggressive; combine with smaller and less aggressive mbuna species.

Water Chemistry: Hard and alkaline; pH 7.6-8.6; GH 7° plus; KH 10-12°

Feeding: Feeds on algae and the small organisms within it. Provide a varied diet which includes a vegetable component such as vegetable and spirulina-based flakes.

Sexing: Juveniles of this species are a solid bright yellow. At around 4cm (1.5in), males turn darker, with blue vertical stripes (much like *Ps. demasoni*).

Breeding: Mouthbrooder. Breeding males will defend territory.

CICHLIDAE (Cichlids)
Pseudotropheus socolofi
POWDER-BLUE CICHLID, PINDANI

10cm
4˝

23-28°C
73-82°F

120cm
48˝

Origin: Africa – Lake Malawi (Mozambique)

Tank Setup: Provide plenty of rocks to form caves.

Compatibility/Aquarium Behaviour: One of the less aggressive mbuna; combine with other similar mbuna species.

Water Chemistry: Hard and alkaline; pH 7.6-8.6; GH 7° plus; KH 10-12°

Feeding: Herbivorous; feed lots of vegetables.

Sexing: The sexes display identical colouration, but males tend to have larger eggs spots in greater numbers than females, as well as longer ventral fins.

Breeding: Mouthbrooder. Breeding males will defend a territory.

CICHLIDAE (Cichlids)
Nimbochromis venustus
GIRAFFE CICHLID, GIRAFFE HAP

25cm
10˝

23-28°C
73-82°F

150cm
60˝

Origin: Africa – widely distributed in Lake Malawi.

Tank Setup: A large tank with plenty of open swimming space and rocks in the background.

Compatibility/Aquarium Behaviour: Predatory; will eat small fish. Aggressive particularly towards its own species and those similar to it including other *Nimbochromis*.

Water Chemistry: Hard and alkaline; pH 7.6–8.6; GH 7° plus; KH 10-12°

Feeding: Cichlid pellets and flakes, supplement with meaty frozen or live food.

Sexing: Males are larger and develop more yellow colouration on their bodies and blue on their heads.

Breeding: Mouthbrooder.

CICHLIDAE (Cichlids)

Altolamprologus compressiceps
NO COMMON NAME IN WIDESPREAD USE

| 10-15cm | 24-27°C | 90cm |
| 4-6″ | 75-81°F | 36″ |

Origin: Africa – widely distributed in Lake Tanganyika.

Tank Setup: Create piles of rocks to break up territories. You can also add shells. It is preferable to use a sand or fine-gravel substrate.

Compatibility/Aquarium Behaviour: Keep with similar sized Tanganyikan cichlids which are not overly aggressive such as *Julidochromis*, medium-sized *Neolamprologus* and *Cyprichromis*.

Water Chemistry: Hard and alkaline; ideal conditions would be pH 7.8-9.0; GH 10-14°; KH 12-18° (see comments for *Neolamprologus brichardi*.)

Feeding: Prefers frozen or live food, but eats most aquarium food.

Sexing: No differences in the sexes are apparent in juveniles, but males are usually significantly larger in established pairs. Mature males also appear deeper bodied with more elongated finnage.

Breeding: Substrate spawner; the female usually selects a cave with a very narrow entrance. The female guards the eggs and fry until they are free-swimming.

Size: Up to 15cm (6in); females are smaller at approximately 10cm (4in).

CICHLIDAE (Cichlids)

Cyphotilapia frontosa
FRONTOSA

| 25-35cm | 24-27°C | 150cm |
| 10-14″ | 75-81°F | 60″ |

Origin: Africa – Lake Tanganyika

Tank Setup: A large tank with plenty of open space, and caves made by carefully stacking large smooth rocks, or using ceramic or PVC pipes.

Compatibility/Aquarium Behaviour: Not overly aggressive for its size; keep with other large fish that can hold their own but are not too aggressive. The open-water Haplochromine cichlids from Lake Malawi are suitable. May eat smaller fish, although not particularly predatory when well fed in the aquarium.

Water Chemistry: Hard and alkaline; ideally pH 7.8-9.0; GH 10-14°; KH 12-18°

Feeding: In the wild, these fish are primarily piscivores (fish eaters), feeding mainly on *Cyprichrominid* cichlids. Provide baitfish such as whitebait, lance fish and silversides, as well as mussels, prawn/shrimp and earthworms. Vary the diet with cichlid sticks and pellets.

Sexing: Males and older females tend to have large nuchal humps on their foreheads. Males also tend to be larger than females. There are no reliable differences in small juveniles.

Breeding: Establish a breeding colony with one male per three to four females. Groups in a large tank tolerate other subdominant males. Spawning is not as aggressive as in other cichlid species. The female mouthbroods for more or less five weeks. Remove and raise the fry separately.

CICHLIDAE (Cichlids)
Cyprochromis leptosoma
NO COMMON NAME IN WIDESPREAD USE

12,5cm
5″

23-26°C
73-79°F

120cm
48″

Origin: Africa – Lake Tanganyika

Tank Setup: A large and deep tank with plenty of open swimming space in the upper levels.

Compatibility/Aquarium Behaviour: Generally peaceful; can keep this species with other Tanganyikan cichlids that occupy rocky habitats in the lower areas of the tank.

Water Chemistry: Hard and alkaline; ideally pH 7.8-9.0; GH 10-14°; KH 12-18°

Feeding: Omnivorous; feed flakes and live and frozen food.

Sexing: Males are more colourful than females, most having blue dorsal and anal fins and a yellow caudal fin.

Breeding: Ideally, keep several females for each male. Spawning takes place in open water near the surface. The female will catch the eggs, which hatch in approximately three weeks. There is no parental care of the fry after release.

CICHLIDAE (Cichlids)
Julidochromis marlieri
CHEQUERED JULIE

15cm
6″

24-27°C
75-81°F

90cm
36″

Origin: Africa – Lake Tanganyika

Tank Setup: Create a pile of rocks for each pair or group of fish, to allow for separate territories.

Compatibility/Aquarium Behaviour: Ideally, keep this species with similar sized Tanganyikan cichlids such as *Neolamprologus*, *Altolamprologus* and (in tall tanks) shoaling *Cyprichromis* species. Established pairs will become very aggressive towards other *Julidochromis*.

Water Chemistry: Hard and alkaline; ideally pH 7.8-9.0; GH 10-14°; KH 12-18°

Feeding: Micropredator: feed flakes or granular food and supplement with plenty of frozen and live food.

Sexing: There are no obvious differences between the sexes. Males have a noticeable genital papilla, and in this species, it is the female which tends to be larger in an established pair.

Breeding: A cave spawner. You can use smooth rocks or plant pots for the spawning cave. The parents guard the eggs and fry.

Cichlidae (Cichlids)
Neolamprologus brichardi
LYRETAIL CICHLID, FAIRY CICHLID

10cm
4″

24-27°C
75-81°F

60cm
24″

Minimum Recommended Tank Size: 60cm (24in) for a single pair, larger if part of a Tanganyikan community.

Origin: Africa – widely distributed in Lake Tanganyika

Tank Setup: Rocky décor; you can include plants tolerant of hard and alkaline water. Construct piles of rocks for each pair of fish or similar species to allow separate territories.

Compatibility/Aquarium Behaviour: Territorial, especially when breeding. Best kept with other similar sized Tanganyikan cichlids such as *Julidochromis* and *Altolamprologus*.

Water Chemistry: Hard and alkaline; pH 7.8-9.0. Precise hardness values are not critical, but always keep pH alkaline (approximate values of Lake Tanganyika would be GH 10-14° and KH 12-18°) to ensure health, and successful breeding.

Feeding: Flakes and granular food; supplement with frozen or live food.

Sexing: Adult males are larger and have more extended finnage than females; no apparent differences in juveniles.

Breeding: Easy to breed in the right conditions. Both parents protect the spawning area. Several generations of fry co-exist.

CICHLIDAE (Cichlids)
Neolamprologus leleupi
LEMON CICHLID

10cm
4″

24-27°C
75-81°F

48cm
120″

Origin: Africa – Lake Tanganyika

Tank Setup: Rocky tank with sand substrate.

Compatibility/Aquarium Behaviour: Very aggressive towards others of its own species. Keep with similar sized Tanganyikan cichlids that are not too similar in body shape.

Water Chemistry: Hard and alkaline; ideally pH 7.8-9.0; GH 10-14°; KH 12-18°

Feeding: Carnivorous – will accept most aquarium foods; include some frozen or live food in the diet.

Sexing: No obvious differences between the sexes.

Breeding: Spawns in caves. The female lays approximately 100 adhesive eggs and guards them. The male may guard the territory, but the pair bond is not usually long lasting, so the tank should be large enough for the female to keep out of sight of the male.

CICHLIDAE (Cichlids)
Symphysodon sp.
DISCUS

15cm
6″

26-30°C
79-86°F

90cm
36″

Origin: South America – Amazon River basin

Tank Setup: A large and fairly deep tank with subdued lighting and gentle water circulation.

Compatibility/Aquarium Behaviour: Peaceful, although the fish will establish a pecking order among themselves. Keep them in a species tank or with other peaceful fish with similar requirements, such as medium-sized tetras, *Corydoras* catfish and dwarf cichlids.

Water Chemistry: Soft and acidic; prefers a pH of 6.0–6.5, although they can withstand slightly hard and alkaline water without problems.

Feeding: Carnivorous; eats live, frozen and granular foods, as well as flakes.

Sexing: The only definitive means of sexing is the genital papilla, which is pointed in males and rounded in females.

Breeding: The female lays eggs on a pre-cleaned spawning site and the parents protect them and the fry. The fry initially feed on body mucous secreted by the parents.

CICHLIDAE (Cichlids)
Thorichthys meeki
FIREMOUTH

15cm
6″

21-25°C
70-77°F

90cm
36″

Origin: North and Central America – Mexico, Guatemala and Belize

Tank Setup: Rounded rocks, wood for cover with a few robust plants and some open space for swimming and displaying.

Compatibility/Aquarium Behaviour: Not overly aggressive, but not usually suitable for the general community tank. Can be kept with larger and more robust fish such as medium-sized barbs and other cichlids of a similar temperament.

Water Chemistry: Neutral to alkaline (pH 7.0-7.5); medium hard.

Feeding: Omnivorous; Cichlid pellets, flakes and granular food; supplement with frozen or live food.

Sexing: Males are larger than females and have more colour, showing more red on their bodies, and have extended dorsal and anal fins.

Breeding: The female normally lays the eggs on a pre-cleaned rock. Both parents tend the fry.

CICHLIDAE (Cichlids)
Uaru amphiacanthoides
UARU/WAROO, TRIANGLE CICHLID

25cm
10˝

24-28°C
75-82°F

120cm
48˝

Origin: South America – Amazon River basin

Tank Setup: A fairly large and deep tank with tall plants around the edges; leave plenty of open swimming space. Subdued lighting is preferable.

Compatibility/Aquarium Behaviour: Peaceful for a cichlid, keep in groups (though males in particular are territorial with their own kind) in a suitably large tank with non-aggressive fish.

Water Chemistry: Fairly soft; prefers neutral to slightly acidic water, captive-bred fish are more tolerant.

Feeding: Omnivorous; feed with flakes and granular, frozen or live food. Also include some vegetable matter.

Sexing: No obvious differences between the sexes.

Breeding: It is best to allow pairs to form from a group. They usually select a hard and smooth spawning site. The parents produce body mucus on which the fry feed initially; they are not particularly vigorous in their defence of the fry.

CICHLIDAE (Cichlids)
Vieja maculicauda
BLACK BELT CICHLID

25cm
10˝

22-26°C
72-79°F

150cm
60˝

Origin: Central America – Guatemala to Panama

Tank Setup: A large tank with robust décor such as rounded stones and large pieces of bogwood. The species is likely to eat or uproot plants.

Compatibility/Aquarium Behaviour: Very aggressive towards their own kind and other species. You could include robust shoaling species to reduce aggression between a spawning pair.

Water Chemistry: Hard and alkaline, but exact parameters not critical; often enters brackish water in the wild.

Feeding: Herbivorous; provide a varied diet with plenty of vegetables.

Sexing: There are no clear differences between the sexes, but males are larger and may be more colourful than females.

Breeding: A substrate spawner that usually chooses a flat rock as a spawning site, where the female may lay several hundred to more than a thousand eggs.

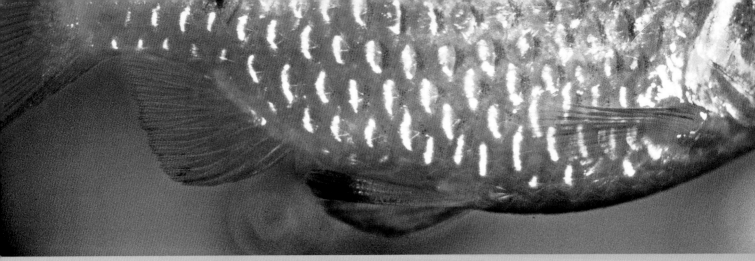

Cyprinids

The Order Cypriniformes contains the large Cyprinidae family, which includes many popular aquarium fish such as barbs, danios, rasboras and 'sharks'. In addition, several families of loaches belong to this order, with the popular aquarium species belonging mainly to the family Cobotidae. The majority of popular Cyprinid fish come from Southeast Asia and the Indian subcontinent, although they are also found in Africa, North America and Europe.

The barbs and danios are frequently among the first fish encountered by new fishkeepers, not least of all because they are usually hardy species that are often the first to be added to new aquaria. The freshwater 'sharks' are also popular, partly due to similarities in their appearance to marine sharks (to which they are not closely related in any way). Some of these species are however extremely territorial towards their own kind and similar fish.

A number of species of loaches are also very popular as aquarium fish, some of them for their ability to reduce snail populations in the aquarium, and a few for their algae-eating abilities.

COBITIDAE (Loaches)
Botia striata
ZEBRA LOACH, CANDY-STRIPE LOACH

7,5cm
3″

23-26°C
73-79°F

75cm
30″

Origin: Southern India

Tank Setup: Planted tank with bogwood or rocks for hiding places; preferably a sand substrate.

Compatibility/Aquarium Behaviour: Generally peaceful in the community tank. More active when kept as a group, which results in some harmless chasing behaviour. You can keep this species with other peaceful loaches.

Water Chemistry: Fairly soft to medium hard; slightly acidic to alkaline (pH 6.5-7.8).

Feeding: Omnivorous – flakes and granular food; supplement with frozen or live food. Eats snails.

Sexing: Unknown

Breeding: Unknown

COBITIDAE (Loaches)
Chromobotia macracanthus
– previously known as Botia macracanthus
CLOWN LOACH

30cm
12″

24-30°C
75-86°F

15cm
6″

Origin: Southeast Asia – Borneo and Sumatra

Size: Up to 30cm (12in), but usually smaller in aquaria.

Tank Setup: Provide plenty of hiding places, as this fish likes to spend some daylight hours hidden away, and will often wedge itself into small gaps in wood or rocks.

Compatibility/Aquarium Behaviour: A normally peaceful community fish that mixes well with fish of varying sizes. This is a sociable loach – keep in a group.

Water Chemistry: Fairly soft; prefers slightly acidic to neutral (pH 6.0-7.0) water, but will adapt to harder and more alkaline water.

Feeding: Omnivorous, but prefers meaty foods such as bloodworms. Will eat most aquarium food.

Sexing: Differences between the sexes unknown, but females may be fuller bodied.

Breeding: Although the Clown Loach is now bred commercially on fish farms in large numbers, there have only been reports of occasional spawnings in aquaria, of which there are no details.

115

COBITIDAE (Loaches)
Pangio kuhlii
KUHLI LOACH
– OFTEN WRITTEN INCORRECTLY AS *'COOLIE LOACH'*.

10cm
4″

21-25°C
70-77°F

60cm
24″

Origin: Southeast Asia namely Borneo, Sumatra, Thailand and Malay Peninsula.

Tank Setup: Soft, sandy substrate. Other décor could include small stones and pieces of wood, and live or artificial plants.

Compatibility/Aquarium Behaviour: A peaceful bottomfeeder; keep in a group.

Water Chemistry: Not critical, but fairly soft and slightly acidic water would be ideal.

Feeding: Omnivorous; prefers small frozen and live food.

Sexing: Differences between the sexes unknown.

Breeding: Accomplished occasionally, but details are sketchy.

COBITIDAE (Loaches)
Yasuhikotakia sidthimunki
— *previously known as Botia sidthimunki*
CHAIN LOACH

10cm
4″

24-28°C
71-81°F

60cm
24″

Origin: Thailand, Cambodia, Laos

Size: 10cm (4in), often smaller in aquaria, but there have been reports of wild-caught specimens being up to 15cm (6in).

Tank Setup: A planted tank with a sandy substrate would be ideal, with a few small stones or pieces of wood to complete the décor.

Compatibility/Aquarium Behaviour: A peaceful species, ideal for the community aquarium. Keep in a group.

Water Chemistry: Soft and slightly acidic water would be ideal, but the farm-bred stock now available is likely to tolerate a wider range of water parameters.

Feeding: Omnivorous; prefers small frozen and live food.

Sexing: Differences between the sexes unknown.

Breeding: No reports of breeding in home aquaria.

CYPRINIDAE (Carps and Minnows)
Balantiocheilos melanopterus
SILVER SHARK, BALA SHARK, TRICOLOUR SHARK

35cm
14″

22-28°C
72-82°F

120cm
48″

Origin: Southeast Asia namely Borneo, Sumatra, Thailand and Malay Peninsula.

Size: Up to 35cm (14in), but usually smaller in aquaria — approximately 15-20cm (6-8in).

Tank Setup: A large tank is required with plenty of swimming space and no sharp décor. Tall plastic or real plants and you can use wood to provide some cover.

Compatibility/Aquarium Behaviour: A very peaceful fish despite the large size it can attain. Territorial fish such as Red-tailed Black Sharks may harass this species. Has a nervous disposition and may jump or crash into décor if startled.

Water Chemistry: Fairly soft, slightly acidic (pH 6.5-7.0) would be ideal, but does fine in harder and more alkaline water.

Feeding: Omnivorous; will eagerly consume the offering of almost any food. Add vegetables to the diet.

Sexing: Differences between the sexes unknown, females may be heavier bodied than the males.

Breeding: Rare in aquaria.

CYPRINIDAE (Carps and Minnows)
Barbonymus schwanenfeldii
— known under many synonyms
TINFOIL BARB

35cm
14″

22-25°C
72-77°F

150cm
60″

Origin: Asia — Thailand, Malay Peninsula, Borneo, Sumatra

Tank Setup: A large tank with plenty of swimming space and artificial or very robust plants; the species will eat live plants.

Compatibility/Aquarium Behaviour: Not aggressive and make good companions for other species of large non-aggressive fish in suitably sized display aquaria. May eat very small fish.

Water Chemistry: Fairly soft, slightly acidic (pH 6.5-7.0) water ideal, but tolerates a range of water parameters well.

Feeding: Herbivorous, but accepts most food.

Sexing: No obvious differences between the sexes.

Breeding: An egg-scatterer. No reports of aquarium breeding, though the species has been bred commercially.

CYPRINIDAE (Carps and Minnows)
Crossocheilus siamensis
SIAMESE ALGAE EATER

| 15cm | 24-26°C | 90cm |
| 6″ | 75-79°F | 36″ |

Origin: Southeast Asia

Tank Setup: Planted community tank.

Compatibility/Aquarium Behaviour: Not aggressive towards other species, and hence suitable for the community tank; less aggressive than some of its look-alikes.

Water Chemistry: Fairly soft, slightly acidic to neutral water ideal, but tolerates hard water well.

Feeding: Omnivorous; a good algae eater; add some vegetables to the diet.

Sexing: Differences between the sexes unknown; females may be deeper bodied than the males.

Breeding: No reports of aquarium breeding.

CYPRINIDAE (Carps and Minnows)
Cyclocheilichthys janthochir
RED-FIN SILVER SHARK, RED-FIN RIVER BARB

| 20cm | 23-26°C | 120cm |
| 8″ | 73-79°F | 48″ |

Origin: Asia – Indonesia

Tank Setup: Use wood and tall live or plastic plants for décor, leaving plenty of open-water swimming space.

Compatibility/Aquarium Behaviour: An active, but generally peaceful shoaling fish.

Water Chemistry: Soft and slightly acidic water ideal, but not critical.

Feeding: Omnivorous; feed a variety of dry aquarium food; supplement with frozen or live food.

Sexing: Females may be larger and deeper-bodied than males.

Breeding: No reports of breeding in aquaria.

CYPRINIDAE (Carps and Minnows)
Danio albolineatus
PEARL DANIO

6cm
2,5″

20-26°C
68-79°F

75cm
30″

Origin: Asia – widespread

Tank Setup: Décor not overly important as this fish spends most of its time at the surface and does not usually seek cover. You can add some tall plants, however.

Compatibility/Aquarium Behaviour: An active shoaling fish that you should keep in a group. Ideal community fish.

Water Chemistry: Not critical, thrives in a range of conditions.

Feeding: Omnivorous; feed flakes and granular, frozen and live food.

Sexing: Males tend to be more colourful than females, which are larger and rounder in shape.

Breeding: Maintain a temperature at the upper end of the range. Female scatters the eggs over fine-leaved plants. Remove the adults immediately after spawning to prevent them from eating the eggs.

CYPRINIDAE (Carps and Minnows)
Danio rerio
ZEBRA DANIO

6cm
2,5″

18-25°C
64-77°F

75cm
30″

Origin: Asia – Pakistan, India, Bangladesh, Nepal and Myanmar

Tank Setup: Planted tank, with open swimming space.

Compatibility/Aquarium Behaviour: An excellent community fish and a very active swimmer.

Water Chemistry: Not critical for this hardy species.

Feeding: Accepts most aquarium food.

Sexing: Females have rounder shapes than the males and are usually slightly larger.

Breeding: Fairly easy to breed; maintain a temperature at the upper end of the scale and keep the water fairly soft. Breed as a pair in a tank with fine-leaved plants, among which the female scatters the eggs. Remove the adults immediately after spawning to prevent them from eating the eggs. Eggs hatch in about 48 hours.

CYPRINIDAE (Carps and Minnows)
Epalzeorhynchos bicolor
RED-TAILED BLACK SHARK

12,5cm
5″

22-26°C
72-79°F

90cm
36″

Origin: Southeast Asia – Thailand. All fish available are captive bred, as this species is extinct in the wild.

Tank Setup: Provide plenty of décor in the way of plants, bogwood and rocks.

Compatibility/Aquarium Behaviour: Territorial and often aggressive, especially to similar-looking fish, which you should not add to the tank. Combine with robust fish that occupy the upper levels of the tank such as barbs, danios and rainbowfish.

Water Chemistry: Prefers fairly soft, slightly acidic water (pH 6.5-7.0), but tolerates more alkaline water well.

Feeding: Omnivorous; eats some algae. Add vegetables, flakes and frozen or live food to the diet.

Sexing: Differences between the sexes unknown; males may have more pointed dorsal fins than females.

Breeding: No detailed reports. Due to aggression, breeding is achieved only occasionally in aquaria.

CYPRINIDAE (Carps and Minnows)
Epalzeorhynchos frenatum and Epalzeorhynchos munense
RED-FINNED SHARK, RUBY SHARK, RAINBOW SHARK

15cm
6″

22-26°C
72-79°F

90cm
36″

Origin: Southeast Asia – Thailand, Laos

Tank Setup: Planted tank with caves of bogwood and/or rocks.

Compatibility/Aquarium Behaviour: Territorial, and can be aggressive. As with the Red-tailed Black Shark, this aggression is more likely to be targeted at others of its own species or similar-looking fish.

Water Chemistry: Prefers fairly soft, slightly acidic water (pH 6.5-7.0).

Feeding: Omnivorous; add vegetables to the diet; will also graze on algae.

Sexing: Males have slimmer body profiles than females.

Breeding: Only occasionally achieved in aquaria – aggression is a problem.

CYPRINIDAE (Carps and Minnows)
Epalzeorhynchos kalopterus
FLYING FOX

| 15cm | 24-26°C | 90cm |
| 6˝ | 75-79°F | 36˝ |

Origin: Malay/Thailand peninsulas and Indonesia

Tank Setup: Planted tank with plenty of décor.

Compatibility/Aquarium Behaviour: Territorial with its own kind. Can keep it in a community tank with other species of fish, that can tolerate its sometimes boisterous behaviour, such as robust barbs.

Water Chemistry: Prefers fairly soft, slightly acidic (pH 6.5-7.0) water, but not essential.

Feeding: Omnivorous; include vegetables in the diet.

Sexing: Differences between the sexes unknown.

Breeding: No reports of aquarium breeding.

CYPRINIDAE (Carps and Minnows)
Leptobarbus hoevenii
CIGAR SHARK, RED-FINNED RIVER BARB

| 100cm | 23-26°C | 180cm |
| 39˝ | 73-79°F | 72˝ |

Size: Up to 100cm (39in), but 45cm (18in) is more likely in home aquaria.

Origin: Asia – Thailand to Sumatra and Borneo

Tank Setup: Requires plenty of open swimming space, with a reasonable water current. You can use large pieces of wood and tall plants to provide décor.

Compatibility/Aquarium Behaviour: A shoaling fish that is not aggressive and should mix well with other large species such as Tinfoil Barbs.

Water Chemistry: pH around neutral; fairly soft to medium-hard.

Feeding: Omnivorous; include vegetables in the diet.

Sexing: Differences between the sexes unknown.

Breeding: Not reported in aquaria.

CYPRINIDAE (Carps and Minnows)
Puntius conchonius
ROSY BARB

| 12,5cm | 18-23°C | 90cm |
| 5″ | 64-73°F | 36″ |

Origin: Asia namely Afghanistan, Pakistan, India, Nepal and Bangladesh.

Tank Set-up: A planted tank with plenty of swimming space.

Compatibility/Aquarium Behaviour: It is preferable to keep this species with other lively community species; it may harass or nip slow-swimming fish with long fins.

Water Chemistry: Fairly soft; around neutral (pH 6.5-7.5).

Feeding: Omnivorous; feed flakes, granular, frozen and live food.

Sexing: Males have more red on their bodies than females.

Breeding: A typical egg-scatterer; remove the adults to prevent them from eating the eggs. Use two females per male.

CYPRINIDAE (Carps and Minnows)
Puntius denisonii
RED-LINE TORPEDO BARB

| 15cm | 18-25°C | 120cm |
| 6″ | 64-77°F | 48″ |

Origin: India

Tank Setup: Large tank with plenty of swimming space; use robust plants. Keep water well oxygenated with a good flow rate.

Compatibility/Aquarium Behaviour: Not usually aggressive; keep with other lively community species.

Water Chemistry: Fairly soft to slightly hard, around neutral (pH 6.5-7.5)

Feeding: Omnivorous; accepts most aquarium foods. It is likely to eat soft-leaved plants.

Sexing: Differences between the sexes unknown.

Breeding: Not reported in home aquaria, but now being commercially bred.

CYPRINIDAE (Carps and Minnows)
Puntius everetti
CLOWN BARB

| 15cm 6″ | 24-29°C 75-84°F | 90cm 36″ |

Origin: Asia – Borneo and Sumatra

Tank Setup: Use rocks, wood and robust plants around the edges, leaving plenty of open swimming space.

Compatibility/Aquarium Behaviour: A lively barb; do not house with timid species.

Water Chemistry: Not critical, but fairly soft and slightly acidic water would be ideal.

Feeding: Omnivorous; feed flakes, granular and frozen or live foods, and include a significant amount of vegetables.

Sexing: Males are generally brighter in colour, and slimmer than females.

Breeding: Egg-scatterer; use soft water at the upper end of the temperature range.

CYPRINIDAE (Carps and Minnows)
Puntius lateristriga
SPANNER BARB

| 18cm 7″ | 24-27°C 75-81°F | 90cm 36″ |

Origin: Asia – Malay Peninsula to Borneo

Tank Setup: You can use rocks, wood and robust plants; leave plenty of open swimmingspace.

Compatibility/Aquarium Behaviour: A boisterous species that you should keeptwith similarly lively species. Older specimens are not as inclined to shoal with each other.

Water Chemistry: Not critical, but fairly soft and slightly acidic to neutral water would be ideal.

Feeding: Omnivorous; feed flakes, granular and frozen or live food, and include a significant amount of vegetables.

Sexing: Males are slimmer in shape than females.

Breeding: Typical egg-scatterer.

CYPRINIDAE (Carps and Minnows)
Puntius nigrofasciatus
BLACK RUBY BARB

6cm
2,5″

21-26°C
70-79°F

75cm
30″

Origin: Asia – Sri Lanka

Tank Setup: Planted tank with open swimming spaces. Avoid overly bright lighting, or provide shade with floating plants.

Compatibility/Aquarium Behaviour: A lively, but normally peaceful, community fish. Keep in a shoal.

Water Chemistry: Fairly soft and slightly acidic (pH 6.5-7.0) water would be ideal, but is not essential.

Feeding: Omnivorous; feed flakes and granular foods; supplement with frozen or live foods – include vegetables. Eats filamentous algae.

Sexing: Males in breeding condition show the intense red/black colour that gives this species its common name. Males also tend to be a little larger than females, though females have thicker body shapes.

Breeding: For spawning, water should be soft and at the higher end of the temperature range. Spawning usually takes place in the morning, with the female scattering the eggs among plants. If you do not remove the eggs, the adults will eat them. The eggs hatch in about 24 hours and the fry are free-swimming several days later.

CYPRINIDAE (Carps and Minnows)
Puntius pentazona
PENTAZONA BARB, FIVE-BANDED BARB

7,5cm
3″

23-26°C
73-79°F

60cm
24″

Origin: Southeast Asia – Borneo, Malay Peninsula, Singapore

Tank Setup: A well-planted tank with plenty of cover for this timid shoaling species. Avoid overly bright lighting, or provide shade.

Compatibility/Aquarium Behaviour: A very peaceful community fish, which may be timid in the presence of more boisterous fish. Keep in a shoal.

Water Chemistry: Prefers fairly soft, slightly acidic water (pH 6.0-7.0).

Feeding: Omnivorous; accepts most foods, but prefers small frozen or live food.

Sexing: Males tend to be more colourful and are smaller and slimmer than females.

Breeding: Use soft and acidic water and maintain the breeding tank at the upper end of the temperature range. This species is a typical egg-scatterer, but not easy to breed.

CYPRINIDAE (Carps and Minnows)
Puntius tetrazona
TIGER BARB, SUMATRA BARB

7,5cm
3″

20-26°C
68-79°F

75cm
30″

Origin: Asia – Borneo and Sumatra

Tank Setup: Planted tank with plenty of swimming space for this active shoaling species.

Compatibility/Aquarium Behaviour: Fishkeepers often include it in a community tank, but it has a reputation as a fin-nipper. Reduce this tendency by keeping it in a shoal of at least six to eight individuals. However, it is still unwise to keep this species with any slow-swimming fish that have long fins such as male Guppies.

Water Chemistry: Fairly soft, slightly acidic (pH 6.5-7.0) water ideal, but certainly not essential as this species will thrive in harder and more alkaline water.

Feeding: Omnivorous; accepts most food.

Sexing: Males are more colourful, smaller and slimmer than females.

Breeding: Typical egg-scatterer. It may be best to allow pairs to develop from within the shoal. A separate tank is advisable for spawning, so that you can return the adults to the main tank after spawning, to prevent them from eating the eggs.

CYPRINIDAE (Carps and Minnows)
Puntius ticto
TICTO BARB, ODESSA BARB

10cm
4″

14-23°C
57-73°F

75cm
30″

Origin: Widespread in Asia – India, Pakistan, Bangladesh, Nepal, Sri Lanka, Myanmar and Thailand

Tank Setup: A well-planted tank with rocks and bogwood to complete the décor.

Compatibility/Aquarium Behaviour: A peaceful species that should mix well with other similar-sized fish in the community tank.

Water Chemistry: Soft and acidic water ideal, but the species is not too demanding.

Feeding: Omnivorous; feed flakes, frozen and live food.

Sexing: Males in breeding condition have a bright-red horizontal band, and more obvious black markings on their dorsal fins.

Breeding: The female will scatter the eggs over fine-leaved plants. Remove the parents after spawning to prevent them from eating the eggs. The eggs hatch in about 24-36 hours.

CYPRINIDAE (Carps and Minnows)
Puntius titteya
CHERRY BARB

5cm
2″

23-26°C
73-79°F

60cm
24″

Origin: Sri Lanka

Tank Setup: A well-planted tank with some shading from floating plants or overhanging tall stem plants.

Compatibility/Aquarium Behaviour: A peaceful barb that is ideal for the community tank. May be timid if kept with livelier species.

Water Chemistry: Fairly soft to medium-hard water; approximately neutral pH (6.5-7.5)

Feeding: Omnivorous; accepts most food; include vegetables.

Sexing: When breeding, males become a deep cherry red; females are brown-red and fuller-bodied than males.

Breeding: Use soft and acidic water in a breeding tank with fine-leaved plants. Eggs hatch in 24 hours. As with other barbs, parents are likely to eat the eggs if they have the opportunity.

CYPRINIDAE (Carps and Minnows)
Boraras maculatus
PYGMY RASBORA, DWARF RASBORA

2,5cm
1″

24-28°C
75-82°F

60cm
24″

Origin: Asia – Malay Peninsula to Sumatra, Indonesia

Tank Setup: A well-planted tank providing plenty of cover.

Compatibility/Aquarium Behaviour: A peaceful species that is quite timid; do not keep it with more boisterous fish.

Water Chemistry: Prefers soft and slightly acidic water.

Feeding: Flakes, micropellets and small frozen or live food.

Sexing: Males are slimmer and more brightly coloured than females.

Breeding: Use soft and acidic water at the upper end of the temperature range. Spawning takes place over fine-leaved plants. Eggs hatch in approximately 24-36 hours. The fry are very tiny, and consequently difficult to rear.

CYPRINIDAE (Carps and Minnows)
Rasbora caudimaculata
RED SCISSORTAIL, GREATER SCISSORTAIL

15cm	20-26°C	120cm
6″	68-79°F	48″

Origin: Southeast Asia — Malaysia, Indonesia and the lower Mekong basin

Tank Setup: Planted tank with plenty of open swimming space and a tight-fitting cover (this species may jump).

Compatibility/Aquarium Behaviour: A very lively, but peaceful community fish.

Water Chemistry: Prefers fairly soft, slightly acidic (pH 6.0-6.8) water.

Feeding: Omnivorous; accepts most food.

Sexing: Males are more slender than females with yellow colouration on their anal fins.

Breeding: No reports of aquarium breeding, probably similar to other *Rasbora* species.

Feeding your fish

A food commonly used for very tiny fry is infusoria — a culture of microorganisms. You can produce it by leaving some aquarium water in a jar for a week or two with a food source (a piece of fruit or vegetable such as banana skin or potato peel), until the water goes cloudy. There are also liquid suspension foods, available commercially, that have a milky consistency. Good second-stage foods, useful for large fry, include live (or frozen) baby brine shrimp, microworms and commercial powdered fry foods. Local fish clubs, aquatic stores and the internet are good sources of information on how to culture your own live foods or obtain starter cultures.

CYPRINIDAE (Carps and Minnows)
Rasbora trilineata
SCISSORTAIL, THREE-LINE RASBORA

10cm
4″

21-25°C
70-77°F

75cm
30″

Origin: Asia – Mekong and Chao Phraya basins, Malay Peninsula, Sumatra and Borneo

Tank Setup: A planted tank with open swimming space.

Compatibility/Aquarium Behaviour: A lively, but peaceful shoaling fish that is an ideal community-tank candidate.

Water Chemistry: Prefers fairly soft, acidic to slightly alkaline water, but not essential.

Feeding: Omnivorous; feed flakes and granular, frozen and live food.

Sexing: There are no obvious differences between the sexes, but males are slimmer than females.

Breeding: Not easy to breed; use soft and acidic water at the upper end of the temperature range. Females scatter the eggs over fine-leaved plants; remove the parents after spawning.

CYPRINIDAE (Carps and Minnows)
Trigonostigma heteromorpha
– previously known as Rasbora heteromorpha
HARLEQUIN RASBORA

5cm
2″

22-26°C
72-79°F

60cm
24″

Origin: Southeast Asia – Thailand to Sumatra

Tank Setup: A planted tank with shade from floating plants or subdued lighting.

Compatibility/Aquarium Behaviour: Peaceful community fish; keep with other small and peaceful fish.

Water Chemistry: Prefers fairly soft, slightly acidic (pH 6.0-6.5) water.

Feeding: Omnivorous; feed flakes and small frozen and live food.

Sexing: The black region on a male is slightly extended and rounded at the bottom. On a female, there is a straight edge to this black portion. Males are slightly slimmer in groups of mature fish.

Breeding: Use very soft, mature acidic water. Remove parents after spawning; eggs hatch in 24 hours.

GYRINOCHEILIDAE (Algae eaters)

Gyrinocheilus aymonieri

ALGAE-EATER, SUCKING LOACH

25cm
10″

23-28°C
73-82°F

90cm
36″

Origin: Asia – Mekong, Chao Phraya and Mekong basins, and northern Malay Peninsula

Tank Setup: Large community tank with bogwood and rocks for hiding places.

Compatibility/Aquarium Behaviour: May become aggressive, particularly when older. Better suited to large community aquaria with larger and more robust fish. May attempt to suck on the sides of deep-bodied fish like Angelfish and Gouramies.

Water Chemistry: Fairly soft, slightly acidic (pH 6.0-7.0) water ideal, but tolerates harder and more alkaline water well.

Feeding: Omnivorous; will eat most aquarium food; good algae-eater when young.

Sexing: Differences between the sexes unknown.

Breeding: No detailed reports; have been bred commercially.

Killifish

The egg-laying tooth carps are usually referred to in the hobby as Killifish, or just 'Killis'. They are very widespread in their global distribution, but most species come from the tropical regions of Africa and South America.

Some Killifish are known as 'Annual Killis', because their natural life cycle typically lasts less than a year. The adults lay eggs before the dry season, which develop in moist substrates in time for the return of the rainy season. Other Killis (the majority) are non-annual, and have a lifespan of around five years. Very few species of Killifish are commonly available in stores, and they tend to represent a rather specialist niche in the hobby. They are often kept by breeders who communicate via local, national and international clubs. Stored eggs, rather than the fish themselves, are often traded. It is not unusual for the dedicated Killifish keeper to have dozens of small breeding tanks set up for these fish. However, many species can also be kept in community aquaria with appropriate tankmates.

APLOCHEILIDAE (Killifish)
Fundulopanchax gardneri gardneri
STEEL-BLUE KILLIFISH, BLUE LYRETAIL

6cm
2,5″

22-25°C
71-77°F

40cm
16″

Origin: Africa – Nigeria and western Cameroon

Tank Set-up: Planted tank with subdued lighting and gentle circulation.

Compatibility/Aquarium Behaviour: You can keep this species in a community tank, as long as there are no tiny tetras or similar fish. Most serious Killifish keepers/breeders place Killifish in species tanks. Males can be quarrelsome.

Water Chemistry: Soft and acidic (pH 6.0-6.5) water.

Feeding: Omnivorous; eats flakes; supplement with small live and frozen food.

Sexing: Males are more colourful than females.

Breeding: The female will scatter eggs over fine-leaved plants. Hatching takes a little longer in this species – about three to four weeks.

APLOCHEILIDAE (Killifish)
Nothobranchius guentheri
REDTAIL NOTHO, GUENTHER'S NOTHO

6cm
2,5″

22-26°C
72-79°F

40cm
16″

Origin: Africa – endemic to the island of Zanzibar

Tank Setup: You can maintain this species in small planted aquaria when they are not being spawned. It prefers a dark substrate and subdued lighting.

Compatibility/Aquarium Behaviour: This species can be kept in a community tank, as long as there are no tiny tetras or similar fish. Most serious Killifish keepers maintain the fish in species tanks. Males can be quarrelsome.

Water Chemistry: Soft and slightly acidic water.

Feeding: Eats flakes and small granular, frozen or live food.

Sexing: Males are much more colourful than females.

Breeding: This species spawns either as a pair, or in rare cases one male spawns with two to three females. It is a substrate spawner which dives into soft substrate (usually peat moss) to bury its eggs. To mimic natural conditions, where small pools disappear in the dry season, remove peat moss containing the eggs from the tank and partially dry it before bagging and storing it for three months. When you rehydrate the peat in a small tank, the fry should appear within 24 hours. Newly hatched baby brine shrimp or microworms are good first foods for the fry.

Livebearers

The live-bearing tooth carps are simply referred to as 'Livebearers' in the hobby, and are among the most commonly kept aquarium fish, especially by beginners. As their name suggests, these fish give birth to live young rather than laying eggs like the majority of other fish. They originate from the southern states of the USA, through Central and South America, though populations have become established in many other parts of the world.

Four types have become staple fish in the hobby: Guppies, Mollies, Platies and Swordtails. Many captive-bred varieties and hybrids of these fish are available — so much so that the original wild-type fish are rarely seen. In addition to the common cultivated strains there are a number of rarer and more challenging livebearing fish available to the enthusiast.

For many fishkeepers, Livebearers will be their first experience of breeding fish. Most of the common livebearing species breed very easily, and it is not uncommon for tanks to become over-stocked with generations of offspring.

ANABLEPIDAE (Four-Eyed Fish)
Anableps anableps
FOUR-EYED FISH

| 30cm 12″ | 24-28°C 75-82°F | 120cm 48″ |

Size: Up to 30cm (12in), but about 20cm (8in) is more likely in the aquarium.

Origin: South America – Trinidad and Venezuela to the Amazon delta in Brazil

Tank Setup: Ideally, a shallow brackish-water aquarium with roots and branches to simulate a mangrove swamp. Use a tight-fitting cover as the fish may jump.

Compatibility/Aquarium Behaviour: Keep with similar-sized non-aggressive fish as it may eat small surface-dwelling fish.

Water Chemistry: Hard alkaline, or slightly brackish water.

Feeding: Eats most floating food including dry food. Vary the diet with frozen and live food.

Sexing: Males have a gonopodium (modified anal fin) and are smaller than females.

Breeding: Anableps are livebearing fish with an unusual modification: their genital organs are structured to be either right or left-sided. A right-sided male can only mate with a left-sided female, and vice versa. Therefore, it is best to let the fish pair off from a group. Each spawning produces only a few large fry up to 4cm (1.5in).

HEMIRHAMPHIDAE (Halfbeaks)
Nomorhamphus liemi
CELEBES HALFBEAK

| 10cm 4″ | 22-26°C 72-79°F | 75cm 30″ |

Origin: Asia – southern Sulawesi (formerly Celebes)

Tank Setup: Mimic a stream or small-river habitat, with rounded stones, a few pieces of wood for décor and shallow water with a good flow.

Compatibility/Aquarium Behaviour: Combine with other peaceful fish, preferably those that use the lower areas of the aquarium. Keep in groups of ideally one male for every two to three females.

Water Chemistry: Medium-hard and alkaline; pH 7.0-8.0

Feeding: Prefers frozen and live food.

Sexing: The males are smaller and more colourful than the females, and have an andropodium (notched anal fin).

Breeding: Livebearer. The gestation period is about six to eight weeks. About a dozen fry are born, which are quite large – approximately 12-15mm (0.5in). Parents will eat their own fry, so it is best to raise them separately.

POECILIDAE
Poecilia sp.
MOLLY

18cm
7˝

20-26°C
68-78°F

75cm
30˝

Origin: Southern USA and Central America

Tank Setup: A hardwater community aquarium with rocks, well-soaked pieces of wood and tough plants (or artificial types).

Compatibility/Aquarium Behaviour: Generally ok in community aquaria, although you can cater better for their needs in a species tank.

Water Chemistry: Hard and alkaline; pH 7.5-8.5. Can keep this species in brackish water or even full marine conditions if acclimatized slowly.

Feeding: Omnivorous; eats vegetables, algae, flakes, frozen and live food.

Sexing: Males have a large dorsal fin and a gonopodium (modified anal fin).

Breeding: Livebearers; produces up to 80 young approximately every six weeks. Keep two or more females per male.

POECILIDAE
Poecilia reticulata
GUPPY, MILLIONS FISH

6cm
2,5˝

18-26°C
64-79°F

60cm
24˝

Origin: Central America and Brazil

Tank Setup: Lightly planted tank with open swimming space at the front and a few stones for additional décor.

Compatibility/Aquarium Behaviour: A peaceful community fish that you should not mix with boisterous species, or any potential fin-nippers.

Water Chemistry: Medium-hard to very hard; alkaline – pH 7.0-8.5. Can keep in slightly brackish conditions, though this is not possible in a general community tank with less salt-tolerant fish.

Feeding: Omnivorous; flakes, small pellet or granular food; small live and frozen food; include vegetables in diet.

Sexing: Males have longer, more colourful finnage and are smaller than females, which tend to be less colourful. However, the most definitive feature in a male is the gonopodium – a stick-like modified anal fin, instead of the normal rounded anal fin featured on the female.

Breeding: A fish that is prolific and breeds easily. It is advisable to keep two to three females per male to prevent the male inducing stress on specific females. They normally produce approximately 30 young.

POECILIDAE
Xiphophorus helleri
SWORDTAIL

10cm
4″

21-26°C
70-79°F

60cm
24″

Origin: Central America

Tank Setup: Planted community aquarium with open swimming space.

Compatibility/Aquarium Behaviour: Males in particular can be slightly aggressive, but the species is generally compatible as a community fish.

Water Chemistry: Medium hard and slightly alkaline; pH 7.0-8.0

Feeding: Omnivorous; flakes, granular, frozen and live food.

Sexing: Only males have the 'sword' and a gonopodium. Females are larger than the males.

Breeding: It is best to move the female to a separate tank so she can give birth. There may be 20 to 80 or more young, depending on the size of the female.

POECILIDAE
Xiphophorus sp.
PLATY

8cm
3″

18-24°C
64-75°F

60cm
24″

Origin: Central America

Tank Setup: A tank with tall plants at the back; leave open swimming space towards the front.

Compatibility/Aquarium Behaviour: Peaceful and hardy; an ideal community fish.

Water Chemistry: Hard and alkaline (pH 7.0-8.0)

Feeding: Eats any aquarium food; include vegetables.

Sexing: Males have a gonopodium; females are larger than the males.

Breeding: A livebearer that breeds easily, producing approximately 50 young every four to six weeks.

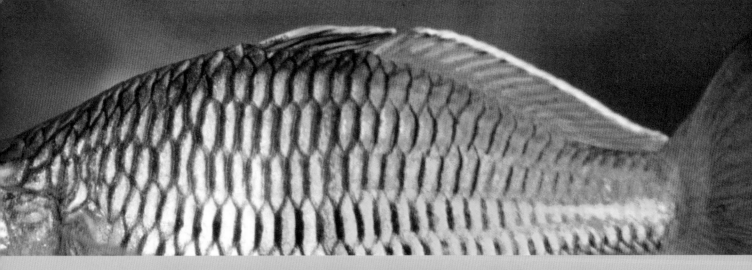

Rainbowfish

Rainbowfish originate mainly from New Guinea and Australia, along with a few species from Madagascar and Southeast Asia.

The species from the family Melanotaenidae are regarded as the 'true' rainbows. The largest genus in this family, Melanotaenia, contains many of the species popular in the hobby and comprises about 50 species in total. Six other genera make up the family. Related families such as the Pseudomugilidae ('blue-eyes') and Atherinidae (silversides) are often referred to as Rainbowfish.

Traditionally, Rainbowfish have not been as popular as many other aquarium fish, such as barbs and tetras. Part of the reason for this may be that juveniles often look somewhat drab, and show little of the stunning adult colouration displayed by many species.

However, in more recent years the popularity of Rainbowfish for aquaria has increased. Most Rainbows are lively, active swimmers that require plenty of open space in the aquarium. They are generally very hardy and adaptable, and thrive in a range of different water chemistries. Although some may be best kept in species tanks, many make good candidates for the community tank.

BEDOTIIDAE (Madagascar Rainbowfish)
Bedotia geayi or Bedotia madagascariensis
MADAGASCAN RAINBOW, RED-TAILED SILVERSIDE

| 15cm | 20-24°C | 120cm |
| 6" | 68-75°F | 48" |

Size: Up to 15cm (6in) reported, though rarely larger than 10cm (4in).

Origin: Endemic to the island of Madagascar, off the coast of East Africa.

Tank Setup: Use rocks, and if desired, well-soaked bogwood along with a few plants. The tank should have clear, well-filtered water with a good flow.

Compatibility/Aquarium Behaviour: An active, but peaceful fish, that should mix well with other similar-sized community fish that share its requirements.

Water Chemistry: Fairly hard and alkaline; pH 7.0-8.0.

Feeding: Omnivorous; feed flakes and granular food; supplement with plenty of frozen or live food.

Sexing: Males are far more colourful than females and have longer first-dorsal fins.

Breeding: Once triggered, spawning will normally take place daily over a period of several months.

MELANOTAENIIDAE (Rainbowfish, blue eyes)
Glossolepis incisus
RED RAINBOW, SALMON-RED RAINBOW

| 15cm | 22-28°C | 120cm |
| 6" | 72-82°F | 48" |

Origin: Indonesia – Lake Sentani, Irian Jaya

Tank Setup: A spacious tank, planted around the edges, with gentle water movement and plenty of open swimming space.

Compatibility/Aquarium Behaviour: A lively, but generally peaceful species, that you should keep in a shoal, and can combine with similar-sized fish in a large community aquarium.

Water Chemistry: Medium hard to hard; neutral to alkaline (pH 7.0-8.5).

Feeding: Omnivorous; feed flakes and granular food; supplement with live and/or frozen food.

Sexing: Breeding males are deep red or reddish brown, females are silvery with a yellowish tinge. Males are deeper-bodied than females.

Breeding: The female spawns over fine plants. Provide either Java Moss or spawning mops. Spawning usually takes place in the morning. The eggs take about seven days to hatch and should be moved to a separate rearing tank.

DATNIOIDIDAE (Tiger-perches)
Datnioides quadrifasciatus
SILVER TIGERFISH, FOUR-BARRED TIGERFISH

30cm
12˝

22-26°C
71-78°F

120cm
48˝

Origin: Asia – India to Indonesia and New Guinea

Tank Setup: A large tank with open swimming space and subdued lighting.

Compatibility/Aquarium Behaviour: Predatory; will eat smaller fish. Can keep in groups of similar-sized individuals in suitably large tanks, although they are territorial towards each other. Peaceful with other large fish.

Water Chemistry: Maintain in slightly brackish conditions or hard and alkaline freshwater.

Feeding: A predator, but can wean it easily onto dead meaty foods such as whitebait, cockles, mussels and prawns or shrimp. Small frozen or live food such as bloodworms are also suitable for juvenile fish.

Sexing: No differences between the sexes known.

Breeding: No reports of aquarium breeding.

GOBIIDAE (Gobies)
Stigmatogobius sadanundio
KNIGHT GOBY

7,5cm
3˝

21-27°C
70-81°F

75cm
30˝

Origin: Asia – India to Indonesia

Tank Setup: Use stones and small pieces of wood to create a number of caves. You can also include plants which grow well in hard and alkaline water, or tolerate lightly brackish conditions.

Compatibility/Aquarium Behaviour: Territorial towards their own kind, so provide plenty of space if keeping a group. You can combine the species with similar-sized fish, but avoid bottom dwelling species that compete aggressively for caves.

Water Chemistry: Hard and alkaline, or slightly brackish water; may fare better in brackish aquaria in the long term.

Feeding: Omnivorous; feed a varied diet including flakes, granular food and pellets; supplement with frozen and live food; also eats some algae.

Sexing: Males have longer anal and second-dorsal fins, and extended fin rays on their first dorsal fins. Females are yellower than males.

Breeding: Maintain temperature nearer the higher end of the range. Displaying and chasing precedes spawning, after which the female lays several hundred eggs, usually in caves, which the male guards.

MASTACEMBELIDAE (Spiny eels)
Mastacembelus erythrotaenia
FIRE EEL

100cm
39˝

24-27°C
75-81°F

150cm
60˝

Size: Up to 100cm (39in), but more often 60cm (24in) in aquaria.

Origin: Asia – Thailand and Cambodia to Indonesia

Tank Setup: Use a soft sandy substrate; provide retreats using pieces of bogwood, PVC or clay pipes. Avoid sharp gravel or any sharp-edged décor. Use a tight-fitting cover, as the fish can escape through small gaps.

Compatibility/Aquarium Behaviour: Not aggressive towards other large fish but will eat small ones. Can be territorial with other spiny eels.

Water Chemistry: Hardness and pH not critical, but water quality must be very high – low nitrates, zero ammonia and nitrite.

Feeding: Carnivorous; earthworms, mussels, prawns/shrimp. Shows no interest in dry foods, and can be initially reluctant to eating older wild-caught specimens. Small juveniles are usually less fussy – you can feed them frozen or live bloodworms and brine shrimp (Artemia).

Sexing: No obvious differences between the sexes, but mature females are thicker bodied than males.

Breeding: Rare in aquaria. Not sexually mature until they exceed 45cm (18in). Females lay eggs in floating plants.

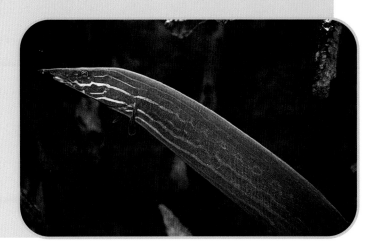

MASTACEMBELIDAE (Spiny eels)
Macrognathus circumcinctus
BANDED SPINY EEL

15cm
6˝

24-27°C
75-81°F

75cm
30˝

Origin: Asia – Mekong and Chao Phraya basins, Thailand, Malayan peninsula and Sumatra

Tank Setup: Provide a soft sand substrate (these fish will often burrow into the substrate with only their heads poking out). You can also use plants, bogwood and PVC or clay pipe to provide cover.

Compatibility/Aquarium Behaviour: Aggressive towards its own kind, but peaceful towards other species. It may only eat fry or very small fish.

Water Chemistry: Not critical – a neutral pH; slightly soft to hard water

Feeding: Small frozen and live food; generally ignores dry food.

Sexing: There are no obvious differences between the sexes.

Breeding: Not reported in aquaria.

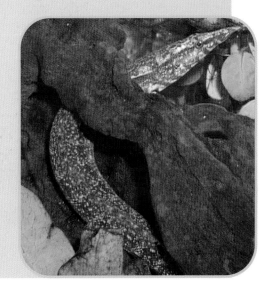

MONODACTYLIDAE (Moonyfish or fingerfish)
Monodactylus argenteus
MONO, MALAYAN ANGEL, MOONFISH

25cm
10″

24-28°C
75-82°F

150cm
60″

Origin: Indo-West Pacific

Tank Setup: A brackish tank with roots or branches; leave plenty of open swimming space. You can use plastic plants – live plants will not tolerate the high salinity requirements for adults.

Compatibility/Aquarium Behaviour: An active shoaling fish that can be aggressive towards its own kind; keep in large numbers of five or more to minimize the potential aggression. It is best to keep this species with other similar-sized robust brackish fish such as Scats and large Archerfish.

Water Chemistry: Hard and alkaline. Often sold in freshwater, but should be adapted to increasingly brackish water as it grows. Adults often live in 100% saltwater.

Feeding: Eats most foods; include some vegetable matter.

Sexing: No obvious differences between the sexes.

Breeding: Only rarely bred in aquaria; changes in salinity are necessary to trigger spawning.

MORMYRIDAE (Elephantfish)
Gnathonemus petersii
ELEPHANTNOSE

20cm
8″

22-28°C
72-82°F

90cm
36″

Origin: Africa – Cameroon, Nigeria, Democratic Republic of Congo (DRC, formerly Zaire)

Tank Setup: Provide plenty of caves for hiding places, and a sandy substrate. Dim lighting is preferable, or provide shade with tall and floating plants.

Compatibility/Aquarium Behaviour: Can be territorial with its own kind. Generally compatible with non-aggressive species in the large community tank.

Water Chemistry: Fairly soft, slightly acidic to neutral (pH 6.0-7.0) water ideal.

Feeding: Omnivorous; prefers live food, but will take frozen food and flakes sometimes.

Sexing: The anal fin of the male is concave.

Breeding: No reports of aquarium breeding.

NOTOPTERIDAE (Featherbacks or knifefish)
Chitala chitala
CLOWN KNIFEFISH

| 120cm 48˝ | 25-28°C 77-82°F | 240cm 96˝ |

Size: Up to 120cm (48in), but not usually more than 60cm (24in) in aquaria.

Origin: Southeast Asia

Tank Setup: A very large tank with open swimming space, gentle circulation and subdued lighting. Preferably use a sand substrate with smooth décor such as rounded stones and bogwood.

Compatibility/Aquarium Behaviour: Highly predatory; this species can be aggressive. Keep with other large fish that are not too aggressive.

Water Chemistry: Not critical, but fairly soft water with a slightly acidic to neutral pH is ideal.

Feeding: Live and frozen meaty food such as whitebait, prawns/shrimp, mussels and earthworms; may also eat pellets which can vary the diet.

Sexing: Differences between the sexes are unknown, but body depth may be an indicator of gender in adult fish.

Breeding: Not bred in aquaria. Spawning takes place on a hard surface and the male guards the eggs and fry.

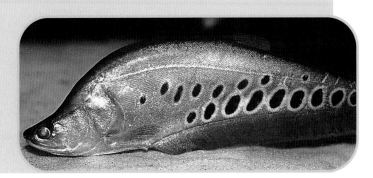

OSTEOGLOSSIDAE (Arowanas)
Osteoglossum bicirrhosum
SILVER AROWANA

| 60cm 24˝ | 24-28°C 75-82°F | 240cm 96˝ |

Size: At least 60cm (24in) in captivity, but can reach 120cm (48in).

Origin: Amazon River basin and the still waters of Guyana

Tank Setup: Very large tank with lots of open swimming space. You could use large pieces of wood and tall plants for décor. A heavy cover is advisable, as these fish are very strong jumpers.

Compatibility/Aquarium Behaviour: Highly predatory; will eat small fish. Some individuals can be aggressive towards other species. Do not keep with very aggressive fish – if harassed, these fish may jump and injure themselves on the aquarium hood or cover glass.

Water Chemistry: Prefers soft and acidic water (pH 6.0-6.9), but tolerates harder water.

Feeding: Carnivorous; eats floating pellets and dead mussels, prawns, whitebait. You can also feed earthworms and crickets.

Sexing: No clear differences between the sexes, though body depth may be an indicator of gender in adult fish.

Breeding: A mouthbrooder, the male carries the eggs for around two months, until the yolk sacs have been absorbed.

OSTEOGLOSSIDAE (Arowanas)
Scleropages formosus
ASIAN AROWANA, DRAGONFISH

90cm 36˝	24-30°C 75-86°F	180cm 72˝

Size: Up to 90cm (36in) reported, but usually smaller in aquaria – approximately 50cm (20in).

Origin: Asia – Cambodia, Indonesia (Kalimantan and Sumatra), Malaysia, Thailand and Vietnam

Tank Setup: A large tank with plenty of open swimming space. Minimal décor.

Compatibility/Aquarium Behaviour: Keep with other very large fish which it cannot swallow. It is best to keep them alone as a specimen fish.

Water Chemistry: Soft acidic (pH 6.0-6.5) water ideal, but the exact pH and hardness are not critical. The water quality must be very high – low nitrates, zero ammonia and nitrite.

Feeding: Carnivorous; live food including fish and insect larvae, will eat dead meaty foods such as mussels and prawns.

Sexing: Differences between the sexes are very difficult to discern. In mature fish, males may be slimmer and possess larger mouths than females, as well as discernable buccal cavities (to incubate eggs).

Breeding: A mouthbrooder, now being bred commercially.

PANTODONTIDAE (Freshwater Butterflyfish)
Pantodon buchholzi
AFRICAN BUTTERFLYFISH

12,5cm 5˝	24-28°C 72-82°F	75cm 30˝

Origin: West and Central Africa

Tank Setup: Some floating and tall plants. Substrate and bottom décor not important, as this fish rarely strays far from the surface; gentle current preferable; tight-fitting lid necessary as this species is a capable jumper.

Compatibility/Aquarium Behaviour: Not aggressive, but may eat small surface-dwelling fish. Do not keep with boisterous fish that occupy the upper levels of the aquarium and certainly not with any potential fin-nippers.

Water Chemistry: Fairly soft water with a slightly acidic to neutral pH is ideal, but not essential.

Feeding: Frozen, live or freeze-dried food that doesn't sink quickly.

Sexing: The male's anal fin is concave on the rear edge, the female's is straight.

Breeding: Soft, acidic water at higher temperature triggers spawning. Females deposit up to 200 eggs in total. When they float to the surface remove to a rearing tank. Fry are difficult to raise and eat tiny food particles.

POLYPTERIDAE (Bichirs)
Erpetoichthys calabaricus
REEDFISH, ROPEFISH, DINOSAUR EEL

90cm 36″	22-28°C 72-82°F	30-90cm 36″

Size: Up to 90cm (36in), usually much smaller in aquaria, approximately 30-40cm.

Origin: West Africa, Cameroon and Nigeria

Tank Setup: Use bogwood, rocks and a few plants, and a sandy substrate. The tank should have a tight-fitting lid or condensation covers, as this fish can escape the aquarium through tiny gaps.

Compatibility/Aquarium Behaviour: Predatory, and may eat small fish. They are peaceful, however, and do not show any aggression towards fish too large to swallow.

Water Chemistry: Not critical – soft to medium-hard; pH 6.0-8.0.

Feeding: Carnivorous; eats live and dead meaty food such as bloodworms, pieces of mussel, prawns/shrimp, baitfish and earthworms. Will also eat catfish pellets, which varies the diet.

Sexing: The anal fins of the males are larger and thicker than those of the females.

Breeding: The female attaches the eggs to plants and other surfaces; they hatch after about three days. The fry will feed on their yolk sacs for the first week.

POLYPTERIDAE (Bichirs)
Polypterus ornatipinnis
ORNATE BICHIR

45cm 18″	25-28°C 77-82°F	150cm 60″

Origin: Central and East Africa – Congo River basin, Lake Tanganyika

Tank Setup: A tank with a large base area (height is less important), with bogwood and smooth rocks for décor. You can include robust plants.

Compatibility/Aquarium Behaviour: Predatory, will eat small fish. Keep with large fish such as Knifefish, Siamese Tigerfish and medium-sized catfish such as *Synodontis*. May bite other bichirs, though no serious damage normally occurs.

Water Chemistry: Not critical – fairly soft to medium-hard; slightly acidic to alkaline.

Feeding: Carnivorous; feed live and dead meaty food such as mussels, prawns/shrimp, earthworms and whitebait; will also eat sinking catfish pellets.

Sexing: Male's anal fin is larger and wider in mature specimens.

Breeding: The male wraps his body around the female's genital area, so that the anal and caudal fins form a cup to receive eggs.

They scatter the adhesive eggs onto plants. The eggs hatch in three to four days. Larvae begin feeding after about a week, when the yolk sac is used up.

POTOMOTRYGONIDAE (River stingrays)
Potamotrygon motoro
OCELLATED STINGRAY

38cm 15″	24-28°C 75-82°F	180cm 72″

Size: Up to 100cm (39in) length recorded in the wild; actual disc size of around 30-38cm (12-15in) is usual for aquarium specimens.

Origin: South America – Orinoco and Amazon river basins

Tank Setup: Substrate of soft sand and minimal décor (smooth stones and pieces of wood); leave plenty of open bottom area.

Compatibility/Aquarium Behaviour: Not for community tanks; will eat small fish. Large and peaceful fish that inhabit the upper levels of the aquarium make good tank mates. Any companions should be fish that will not compete aggressively for food, as this will make feeding the rays difficult.

Water Chemistry: Soft and slightly acidic water is ideal, but tolerates hard water well. Water quality must be excellent, with low nitrates and zero ammonia or nitrite.

Feeding: These fish have big appetites; you should feed them bloodworms, prawns/shrimp, mussesl, baitfish and earthworms.

Sexing: Males have obvious claspers on their pelvic fins, which are used during spawning.

Breeding: Has been bred in captivity quite regularly. Males can become aggressive, and the female may receive bite marks to the outer edges of the disc. After a gestation period of around three months, the swollen female gives birth to live young, which are perfect miniatures of the parents.

PROTOPTERIDAE (African lungfish)
Protopterus annectens
AFRICAN LUNGFISH

60cm 24″	25-30°C 77-86°F	60cm 24″

Size: Up to 100cm (39in), but 60cm (24in) more likely in aquaria.

Origin: Western Africa

Tank Setup: Use rocks or large pieces of bogwood for cover and a sandy substrate (this species can ingest gravel accidentally when feeding). Use a heater guard or an external heater type to prevent burns.

Compatibility/Aquarium Behaviour: These fish can be aggressive and they have a formidable bite so it is preferable to keep them alone.

Water Chemistry: Not important as long as you avoid extremes.

Feeding: Carnivorous; feed mussels, earthworms, baitfish, sinking catfish and pellets.

Sexing: Differences between the sexes unknown.

Breeding: No reports of aquarium breeding. In the wild, this species breeds in burrows at the start of the rainy season. The male remains with the eggs and protects the young initially.

SCATOPHAGIDAE (Scats)
Scatophagus argus
SCAT, SPOTTED SCAT, GREEN SCAT

30cm 12˝ | 23-28°C 73-82°F | 150cm 60˝

Origin: Indo-Pacific

Tank Setup: A large brackish tank with plenty of open swimming space. You can use branches, roots or bogwood for décor, along with artificial plants if you so desire.

Compatibility/Aquarium Behaviour: Semi-aggressive towards its own kind, and is therefore best kept in a group of five to six or more to spread out the aggression. It mixes well with other similar-sized brackish fish such as Monos. Do not keep with more timid fish that will be unable to compete with this boisterous and greedy feeder.

Water Chemistry: Maintain in brackish conditions. You can often buy juveniles in fresh or slightly salted water, but high-end brackish or marine conditions are preferable for adults.

Feeding: Omnivorous; greedily eats any food offerings, so provide a varied diet including plenty of vegetable matter. Will eat live plants.

Sexing: No known differences between the sexes.

Breeding: Not usually accomplished in aquaria, requires a change in salinity to trigger spawning.

TETRAODONTIDAE (Puffers)
Carinotetraodon travancoricus
DWARF PUFFER, PYGMY PUFFER, INDIAN PUFFER

2,5cm 1˝ | 24-26°C 75-78°F | 60cm 24˝

Origin: India

Tank Set-up: Planted tank with live or artificial plants for cover.

Compatibility/Aquarium Behaviour: Despite its small size, it may nip the fins of other fish. It is therefore preferable to keep it in a species tank or with small quick-moving fish that do not have long fins.

Water Chemistry: A freshwater puffer. Fairly soft to slightly hard water; pH 6.5-8.0.

Feeding: Carnivorous; feed small live and frozen food including snails, bloodworms, brine shrimp (Artemia), krill, small pieces of mussel and prawns or shrimp.

Sexing: Mature males feature a brownish line along their stomachs, from their throats towards their anal fins. Females are generally rounder in body shape than males. These differences are not apparent in juveniles.

Breeding: Has been bred in aquaria; few details are available.

TETRAODONTIDAE (Puffers)
Colomesus asellus
SOUTH AMERICAN PUFFER, BRAZILIAN PUFFER

15cm 6″	24-28°C 75-82°F	10cm 4″

Size: 15cm (6in) reported, but more often 10cm (4in) in aquaria.

Origin: Amazon basin – Brazil, Colombia and Peru

Tank Setup: Provide some cover with plants and bogwood or rock caves, with open swimming space.

Compatibility/Aquarium Behaviour: A fairly peaceful puffer, but still inclined to nip fins – do not keep it with any slow-swimming fish with long fins. It does not generally show aggression towards its own species, and you can keep it in such a group.

Water Chemistry: Freshwater species; pH around neutral; fairly soft to medium-hard.

Feeding: Eats live and frozen meaty food – snails, bloodworms and brine shrimp, mussels, prawns/shrimp.

Sexing: Differences between the sexes unknown.

Breeding: No reports of aquarium breeding.

TETRAODONTIDAE (Puffers)
Tetraodon biocellatus
FIGURE-8 PUFFER

7,5cm 3″	24-28°C 75-82°F	75cm 30″

Origin: Asia – Indo-China, Indonesia, Malaysia, Thailand

Tank Setup: Either a species tank, or a community with selected companions. Leave some open swimming space, but provide rocks, bogwood and artificial or salt-tolerant plants for cover.

Compatibility/Aquarium Behaviour: May eat small community fish. Not particularly aggressive, but may still nip fins particularly those of slow-swimming species with long fins. Can keep it in a group of its own species.

Water Chemistry: Ideally kept in brackish conditions. Level of salt is not critical; a specific gravity of around 1.005 will suffice.

Feeding: Feed live and frozen meaty food such as bloodworms, prawns or shrimp, mussels and snails.

Sexing: There are no obvious differences between the sexes.

Breeding: Has been bred in aquaria, but few details are available. The female lays eggs on plants, which the male guards.

TETRAODONTIDAE (Puffers)
Tetraodon fluviatillis
GREEN PUFFER, TOPAZ PUFFER

20cm
8″

24-28°C
75-82°F

120cm
48″

Origin: Asia – Bangladesh, India, Sri Lanka

Tank Setup: A brackish tank with rocks, bogwood or robust or plastic plants for cover.

Compatibility/Aquarium Behaviour: Will eat small fish. Not overly aggressive towards similar-sized fish, including its own kind or other puffers. It is preferable to keep it with larger brackish fish such as monos and scats. Fish added to the aquarium later may be at significantly higher risk than those that the puffer has grown used to.

Water Chemistry: Found in freshwater and brackish habitats; water should be hard and alkaline. These puffers seem to grow faster and be hardier and less disease-prone when kept in brackish water.

Feeding: Eats live and frozen meaty food such as bloodworms, baitfish, cockles, mussels, earthworms and snails.

Sexing: Differences between the sexes unknown.

Breeding: Spawning occurs in brackish water. The female lays the eggs on the substrate or a stone, and the male guards them. Hatching takes about a week.

TETRAODONTIDAE (Puffers)
Tetraodon lineatus
NILE PUFFER, FAHAKA PUFFER, BANDED PUFFER

30cm
12″

24-26°C
75-79°F

120cm
48″

Size: Up to 45cm (18in), but usually smaller in aquaria, approximately 25-30cm (10-12in).

Origin: Africa – Nile, Chad basin, Niger, Volta, Gambia, Geba and Senegal rivers

Tank Setup: A fairly large tank with open swimming space.

Compatibility/Aquarium Behaviour: Usually very aggressive and intolerant of its own species and other fish. It is preferable to keep it alone.

Water Chemistry: pH around neutral; soft to medium hard. A freshwater species that is only found occasionally in slightly brackish water in parts of its habitat.

Feeding: Eats live and frozen meaty food such as cockles, mussels, prawns or shrimp, earthworms and snails.

Sexing: No obvious differences between the sexes. You can observe minor differences in spawning adults.

Breeding: Very rare in aquaria, probably largely due to aggression, which dissuades many people from attempting to breed them.

TETRAODONTIDAE (Puffers)
Tetraodon mbu
GIANT PUFFER

75cm
30˝

24-28°C
75-78°F

180cm
72˝

Minimum Recommended Tank Size: 180cm (72in) x 75cm (30in) x 60cm (24in) for adult fish.

Origin: Africa — Congo River and Lake Tanganyika

Tank Setup: Large tank with plenty of open swimming space; include smooth and robust décor items around the edges.

Compatibility/Aquarium Behaviour: A species with a wide variation in temperament. Most individuals seem oblivious to their tankmates and pay them little attention, others can be aggressive and intolerant of other fish. Formidable teeth could potentially do serious damage. Sheer size alone makes the species unsuitable for the general community tank.

Water Chemistry: A freshwater species; the exact parameters are not critical — fairly soft to hard water with a neutral to alkaline pH.

Feeding: Carnivorous; eats live and frozen food including snails, crabs, mussels, shrimps or prawn and earthworms.

Sexing: Differences between the sexes unknown.

Breeding: Not reported in home aquaria — not practical due to the adult size of this species.

TETRAODONTIDAE (Puffers)
Tetraodon nigroviridis
GREEN SPOTTED PUFFER

15cm
6˝

24-28°C
75-82°F

90cm
36˝

Origin: Asia — India, Indonesia, Sri Lanka, Thailand

Tank Setup: A brackish tank with rocks, bogwood or plastic plants for cover.

Compatibility/Aquarium Behaviour: Will eat small fish and may bite the fins of larger fish. Keep in a species tank or with larger brackish fish such as monos, archerfish and other similar-sized puffers.

Water Chemistry: Brackish; hard and alkaline.

Feeding: Eats live and frozen meaty food such as bloodworms, krill, snails, prawns or shrimp and mussels.

Sexing: Differences between the sexes unknown.

Breeding: Spawning occurs in brackish water. The female lays the eggs on the substrate and the male guards them.

TOXOTIDAE (Archerfish)
Toxotes jaculatrix
ARCHERFISH

25cm
10″

25-30°C
77-86°F

120cm
48″

Origin: India, Southeast Asia to Australia

Tank Setup: An ideal setup would be a mangrove-swamp habitat with the water level several inches below the top of the tank. You can then use branches and overhanging vegetation (real or plastic plants) as an area to introduce insects, allowing the Archer to demonstrate its abilities. You need a tight-fitting cover!

Compatibility/Aquarium Behaviour: Can be aggressive towards its own kind – if you keep more than one such fish, you should introduce three or more similar-sized individuals at the same time. This species is generally peaceful with other similar-sized fish. You can combine it with puffers, gobies and shoaling fish such as monos in a suitably large tank.

Water Chemistry: Fairly hard, neutral to alkaline (pH 7.0-8.5) water. Can often buy this species in freshwater when it is young, but brackish water is beneficial for its long-term health.

Feeding: Insectivorous; feeds from the surface on floating food.

Sexing: No differences between the sexes known.

Breeding: Unknown

Glossary

Absorption Process by which a material is taken up and retained internally, like water in a sponge.

Activated carbon Carbon that has been treated under very high temperature to increase its porosity and hence its ability to adsorb more material from the water.

Adsorption Process by which a solid retains another material on its surface.

Airlift tube A plastic tube used on an undergravel filtration system through which rising air bubbles pass.

Airstone Porous stone used to create fine bubbles from an air pump output.

Biofilm A covering of bacteria, algae and associated material that collects on solid surfaces.

Biofiltration The aspect of filtration that is concerned with the conversion of toxic wastes by bacteria into less toxic forms.

Biotope A natural habitat associated with particular animals and plants.

Brood care Parental care of fry by the adult fish, as occurs with many cichlid fish.

Bubblenest A spawning area created on the surface of the water from bubbles and sometimes plant material.

Carbonate Hardness (KH) A measurement of carbonate and bicarbonate ions in the water that contributes to pH stability or 'buffering capacity'.

Caudal fin The tail fin, used as the main means of propulsion by most fish.

Cycling time The time taken for a new aquarium and filter system to build up enough nitrifying bacteria to convert toxic ammonia and nitrite into nitrate efficiently.

Dechlorinator A chemical agent used to eliminate chlorine from tap water, which is harmful to aquatic organisms.

De-ionized (DI) water Very pure water produced by passing through resins that remove impurities from the water.

Fluidized sand bed A biological filter consisting of a moving bed of sand grains that provides a substrate for baterial colonization.

General Hardness (GH) A measurement of (mainly) calcium and magnesium ions in the water that makes up part of the overall ion content.

Genus A word used for a set of closely related speces that have been placed in the same scientifically-defined group.

Gonopodium The copulatory organ of a male livebearing fish, formed from a modified anal fin.

Grazers Fish that feed in a fairly constant manner on algae, biofilms and the organisms within them.

Hydrogen ions (H+) The chemical ions on which the measurement of pH is based.

Hydrometer A device for measuring the specific gravity or salinity of water.

Ichthyologist A scientist that studies fish.

Infusoria Naturally-occurring tiny organisms that can be cultured for use as food for tiny fry.

Insectivore A species that feeds primarily on insects.

Labyrinth organ An extra organ present in some fish that allows them to take supplementary gulps of air from the surface of the water.

Nocturnal Mainly active and feeding at night.

Omnivore A species that feeds on a range of different foods, which may include plant matter and other animals.

Overflow box or weir A device for straining water from a tank, usually to feed a sump filter beneath the tank.

Papilla A small fleshy tube usually only visible during breeding, through which eggs or the male's milt pass.

Peat Partially decomposed plant matter, which can be used to soften and acidify water.

Piscivore A predatory fish that eats other fish.

Powerhead Water pump that may be used for additional circulation or to power an undergravel filtration system via an uplift tube.

Priming device A useful gadget usually found on external filters to initiate water flow into the filter before switching on the pump.

Quarantine tank An additional aquarium used to hold fish temporarily until they can be deemed healthy and disease-free.

Reverse osmosis (RO) A process of producing pure water by forcing it through a fine membrane that rejects a large percentage of contaminants.

Shoal A group of fish swimming together in a loose manner; a tighter formation swimming in a specific direction is referred to as a school.

Spawning The act of laying and fertilizing eggs.

Spawning mop An artificial (and usually homemade) spawning substrate, normally consisting of wool strands or similar attached to a floating or sinking anchorage point.

Spray bar Device attached to the output tube of a power filter to divide the water flow into several tiny jets of water, to increase aeration.

Swim bladder A specialized organ in fish that provides them with buoyancy.

Taxonomy The science of classifying living organisms.

Venturi attachment A device used on the output of a power filter to introduce air bubbles to the outgoing stream of water.

Index

Associations

AMERICA

American Cichlid Association
43081 Bond Court
Sterling Heights
MI 48313
America
Tel: +1 586 739 1286
Email: cichlids01@wowway.com
Website: www.cichlid.org

CANADA

Canadian Association of Aquarium Clubs
142 Stonehenge Pl.
Kitchener
Ontario
Canada
N2N 2M7
Tel: +1 519 745 1452
Email: miecia@rogers.com
Website: www.caoac.on.ca

UNITED KINGDOM

Catfish Study Group (UK)
Northbank
Drumcross Road
Bathgate
West Lothian
Scotland
EH48 4NT
Email: membershipsecretary@catfishstudygroup.org
Website: www.catfishstudygroup.org

GERMANY

DKG – German Killifish Association
Europaring 24
D-26289 Wilhelmshaven
Germany
Tel: +49 44211 73698
Fax: +49 4421 745514
Email: gerowhv@aol.com
Website: http://dkg.killi.org

AUSTRALIA

Australia New Guinea Fishes Association (ANGFA Inc)
PO Box 673
Ringwood Vic 3134
Australia
Email: membership@angfa.org.au
Website: www.angfa.org.au

NEW ZEALAND

Federation of New Zealand Aquarium Societies
50a Meeanee Road
Taradale
Napier
New Zealand
Tel: +64 6 845 2512
Email: webmaster@fnzas.org.nz
Website: www.fnzas.org.nz

SOUTH AFRICA

South African Koi Keepers Society
PO Box 572
Ferndale
2160
South Africa
Tel/Fax: +27 11 679 3512
Email: sakks@netactive.co.za
Website: www.sakks.co.za

Picture Credits

All photography from www.jjphoto.dk except for those images supplied by photographers or agencies as listed below:

(*key to locations: t=top; b= bottom)

p6-7		Digital Images Solutions (DIS)/Andre Wepener
p12	t	Gallo Images/Gettyimages.com
	b	Digital Images Solutions (DIS)/Andre Wepener
p15		Digital Images Solutions (DIS)/Andre Wepener
p14		Images of Africa (www.imagesofafrica.co.za)
p17		Images of Africa (www.imagesofafrica.co.za)
p19		Tim Martin/Naturepl.com/Photo Access
p21		Images of Africa (www.imagesofafrica.co.za)
p23-24		Images of Africa (www.imagesofafrica.co.za)
p25		Dr Sean Evans
p30	t	Digital Images Solutions (DIS)/Andre Wepener
p30-32		Images of Africa (www.imagesofafrica.co.za)
p36-38		Images of Africa (www.imagesofafrica.co.za)
p40a-b		Dr Sean Evans
p40c		Karen Gowlett-Holmes/Photolibrary.com/Photo Access
p42		Images of Africa (www.imagesofafrica.co.za)
p44		David Hosking/FLPA
p45-46		Images of Africa (www.imagesofafrica.co.za)
p47		Christophe Ratier/NHPA
p48		The Bigger Picture/Photononstop
p49		R. Dirscherl/FLPA
p53		Aaron Norman
p60	t	Aaron Norman
p61	t	Aaron Norman
p71		Aaron Norman
p72	t	Aaron Norman
p84	t	Aaron Norman

p90	b	www.photomax.org.uk
p91	t	Dr Sean Evans
	b	Fabio FG Roselet
p97	b	www.photomax.org.uk
p107	t	Scott W. Michael
	t	Dr Sean Evans
p118	t	Aaron Norman
p119	t	Aaron Norman
p131	t	www.photomax.org.uk
p141	b	Dr Sean Evans
p142	t	Dr Sean Evans
p143	b	Dr Sean Evans
p146	b	Aaron Norman
p149	b	Dr Sean Evans
p151	t	Dr Sean Evans